Looking Back at Pencarrow

by

David Donaldson

Published by
Bodmin Town Museum,
Mount Folly, Bodmin, Cornwall, PL31 2HQ

About the Author

David Donaldson is a retired teacher and headmaster. For the past eight years, he has acted as the honorary archivist of the Molesworth family records held at Pencarrow. He was a founder member of the Friends of Pencarrow, the Chairman when it became a Registered Charity in 2005, and he subsequently served a term as a Trustee of the Charity. His particular interest, and the subject of his doctorate, is the history of the island of Minorca, and he has published articles on this topic in journals both in this country and in Spain.

Cover design by W.H.Johnson. It shows the Coat-of-Arms of Sir William Molesworth, 8th Baronet.

Published by:
Bodmin Town Museum, Mount Folly, Bodmin, Cornwall, PL31 2HQ. Manuscript prepared for publication by W H & J M Johnson, the publishing team.

ISBN-13: 978-0-9549913-7-1

Printed by MPG Books Ltd, Bodmin, Cornwall

Contents

Foreword

An archivist has a formidable challenge. To him falls the unenviable job of sifting through documents, from accounts and legal deeds to photographs and diaries, and extracting the stories of the people they concern. David Donaldson has put countless hours into researching and cataloguing Pencarrow's archives, a much-needed task for which the family is hugely grateful.

His work has yielded a rich vein of stories about my husband's ancestors, who have owned Pencarrow since Elizabethan times, and the many others, from relatives to staff and the wider Cornish community, whose lives were entwined with Pencarrow's.

The year 2010 marks a double milestone for two of the family's most significant members: Sir William Molesworth, the 8th baronet, and his sister Mary Ford. William (born in 1810) and Mary (died in 1910) both left lasting impressions in the gardens, and were benefactors for many local causes.

Reading David's collection of essays gives insight not only into their lives and the history of Cornwall, but the development of Pencarrow in what is arguably the last great epoch of the British stately home.

We thank him and the Friends of Pencarrow for ensuring Pencarrow's past is preserved while we continue with hope into a new century.

Thank you also to Bodmin Town Museum, and to Bill and Janet Johnson for their production expertise.

Iona Molesworth-St. Aubyn
Pencarrow

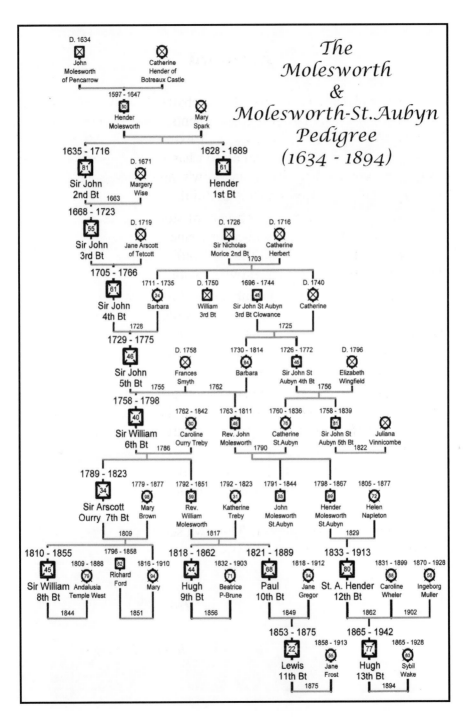

The Molesworth & Molesworth-St.Aubyn Pedigree (1634 - 1894)

5

Engraving (1824) of the south and east fronts of Pencarrow House by F.W.L. Stockdale

Sir William Molesworth, Bart.

His Minority Years 1810-1831

William Molesworth in 1821, aged 11. The only surviving likeness of him as a child.

William was born in May 1810, the eldest child of the marriage (1809) of Sir Arscott Ourry Molesworth and Mary, the eldest daughter of Patrick Brown of Edinburgh and his wife Mary (née Hume), also of Edinburgh, a near relation of David Hume the Scottish philosopher and historian. He was barely into his teens when his father died on Boxing Day 1823, and he succeeded as the 8th baronet. Although the Molesworth seat was at Pencarrow, Sir Arscott and his family stayed there only intermittently during his lifetime. In fact, Sir Arscott did not visit, let alone stay at Pencarrow from the time he succeeded to the baronetcy in 1798 until the summer of 1812 and, even then, John Clift, one of the Pencarrow estate workers, predicted that 'the family will not stay long for the house is not furnished yet.' Sir Arscott was a keen huntsman and when he and his family came to the West Country they seem to have spent more time at Tetcott, the Molesworth estate in north Devon and renowned hunting country, than at their principal residence.

It is possible to trace the movements of the Molesworth family in William's childhood years by the locations in which his mother Mary gave birth to her children - London in 1810 and 1811 for the births of William and Elizabeth respectively; Edinburgh in 1813 for the birth of her twins, Arscott and Caroline, and Tetcott in 1816 and 1818 for the births of Mary and Francis. 1816 must have been a busy and much travelled year for the family: they were at Tetcott in January for Mary's birth, in Edinburgh at some stage for Raeburn to paint Sir Arscott's portrait[1] and yet, as he was High Sheriff for the Duchy in that year, some time will have necessarily been spent in Cornwall. 1817 saw the family in residence at Pencarrow in the early months and again in the autumn and winter, but they stayed there only for weeks at a time in subsequent years until Sir Arscott's death, without any predictable pattern of residence being established.

Details of William's childhood years are limited. There are his own recollections as told to Harriet Grote and briefly recorded by her in an account of his life published in 1866; his mother, Mary, Lady Molesworth's even briefer account written in a letter to her daughter, Mary Ford, shortly after William's death in 1855; an appreciation of William's life written by his brother-in-law, Richard Ford, his sister Mary's husband, based on material provided from memory by Mary and her mother, at about the same time, and a letter written to Lady Molesworth in 1824 by Dr Lecke, William's doctor. These are the sources of the accounts of childhood in the two biographies of William published in the last century, by Millicent Fawcett in 1901, by Alison Adburgham in 1990, but a recently discovered manuscript listing the expenses incurred by William in the year following his father's death sheds a little more light on the way of life of the young baronet.

There are factual discrepancies and inconsistencies in the various descriptions of William's early years, but the accounts tally in the assertion that his poor health dictated the course of his life, even in childhood. He owed his delicate physical constitution to an affliction known as the King's Evil or scrofula, which caused him to suffer fevers, swellings and considerable bodily discomfort. In William's case the illness manifested itself in an infection of his lymph nodes which produced ulcers in his throat, ears and neck which were not only painful but were so disfiguring that, to quote his own words, 'my schoolfellows made sport of me and allowed themselves to use language which cut me to the soul in reference to my deplorable infirmity.'

The schoolfellows to whom William referred were fellow pupils at Mr Carmalt's boarding school in Putney where William was being educated when his father died, and where William himself thought that he was 'ill-cared for and negligently taught.' It had been Sir Arscott's firm intention, to send William to Eton to follow in his, and his own father, the 6th baronet's footsteps, despite the inflammatory diathesis condition with which his son was afflicted and which, if only because it rendered him in his own words 'incapable of mixing youthful exercises and pastimes,' was certain to set him aside from other pupils in any boarding school. After the death of her husband, Lady Molesworth proved more understanding of William's delicate state of health. William returned to Mr Carmalt's school in late January 1824, but his mother sought further medical opinion about William going on to Eton and, by the summer, the following letter from one of the physicians she consulted, persuaded her to follow the advice it contained:

18 June 1824
Dr Lecke has great Pleasure in reporting to Lady Molesworth that Sir William's now in a fit state to join her Ladyship at the Seaside whenever she wishes. As Sir Wm's Constitution is highly susceptible of (? *indecipherable*) will be necessary for him to observe a mild Diet without wine, to be moderate in his exercise & exposure to the Sun in short to avoid all Causes of high excitement both corporal & mental. He may use the tepid Bath every other day at 84 [?] making merely a Plunge in it & perhaps at the end of the Season - in August or September go a few times into the Sea but this should be with the concurrence of some medical Opinion. Sir William's great Vivacity & good Humour combined with no ordinary Talent render some directions of his Pursuits to a right Course highly desirable at his Time of Life. His future Health & Happiness will greatly depend on this. It appears therefore to Dr Lecke part of his duty to suggest to her Ladyship the advantage that must be desired from the immediate assistance of an able Tutor. Boys of fifteen or sixteen are generally above Restraints & Coercion from Females however much they may love & respect them. Often when they are placed at Eton or any other School [they] fall sacrifice to ardent dispositions unless corrected by some Master who takes more than an ordinary interest in their Fate.

William did not go on to Eton from Mr Calmady's school. A Mr Bartholomew was engaged as his tutor, and he accompanied the young baronet to Sidmouth where they stayed for four months. In September 1824, Lady Molesworth decided to return to be close to her own family in Edinburgh, and the Scottish capital remained the family base for the next six years. William and his tutor went north to join them in October, and Lady Molesworth again sought medical opinion about the form William's future schooling should take. Much to the chagrin of William's grandmother, the Dowager Lady Molesworth, his uncle William (his father's younger brother) and his aunt Caroline, who were all in favour of carrying out Sir Arscott's wishes, Dr Lecke's views were supported. Richard Ford recalled that the 'most eminent physician of Edinburgh pronounced that step [boarding school] to be equivalent to signing his death warrant.' William's future education was to follow an individual pattern best suited to his delicate health, his temperament and his intellectual curiosity.

In his letter to Lady Molesworth, Dr Lecke had sent a suggested timetable of study

Scheme
Hours
Monday & following days, Sunday excepted
7-9: 10-2
Bible Studies for the day
One Greek or one Latin Lesson every day
One Latin or English Composition every day
History - a certain portion to be read during the week and examined on Sunday
French - one hour per day
Drawing - every other day in play hours
Greek (?) on Sundays with Mant's Bible

9

for William. It was a basic curriculum for a young man of his standing in the 1820s. It will not have seemed excessively demanding to William, given his self-confessed 'natural leaning to study.' It was certainly not as exacting a schedule as the one he was later to adopt for his studies in Edinburgh and that William had plans for the free time that he was to be allowed is revealed in a letter written by him to Lady Molesworth shortly after Dr Lecke had pronounced him fit to go to Sidmouth:

> 24 June 1824
>
> My dear Mother
> I am very much obliged to you for your kind letter. I have got the pleasure of informing you that I am quite well. I left some book with Miss Dietz which I should like to have and a Italian Grammar likewise my fishing rod which Brighton[2] has. I ride every day. I shall be very glad to see you all well at Sidmouth.
> If there is any fishing tackle tell Cleave[3] to bring it with the rod. Love to all
>
> I am dear Mother
> Your dutiful son
> W. Molesworth.

Among the Molesworth-St. Aubyn papers in the Cornwall County Record Office is *An Account of the Guardian's Expenditure in the Maintenance & Education of Sir William Molesworth Bart., during his Minority.* Regrettably, the account is incomplete: it deals only with expenditure for the calendar year 1824, and principally with expenses incurred at Sidmouth, but it is nevertheless quite informative. William was in receipt of an allowance which provided him with two shillings per week in January which was increased to five shillings by August; he also appears to have received an additional two shillings in pocket money while he was at school in Putney and, at the end of the year, he was given a Christmas bonus of five guineas. We learn that he returned to school from Pencarrow by 'posting' to Goodamoor at Plympton (the home of his paternal grandmother's Treby family), then on by subscription coach to Cobham Lodge, the home in Surrey which Caroline Lady Molesworth shared with her daughter Caroline, before going on to Putney.

It is not known whether the fishing rod and tackle reached William in Sidmouth and, if they did, the extent to which he put them to use, but we know from the *Account,* that he did ride regularly. In early July, John Cleave brought two horses, Button and Rosabelle, from Pencarrow to Bodmin for him to ride. They were stabled at the Sidmouth Inn for nearly ten weeks at a cost of sixteen shillings per week, and he had also to pay the expenses of a farrier (£1.13s.), a saddler (£1.1s.9d.) as well as buying spurs (10s.), a bridle (£1.5s.) and two pairs of chaps (3s.6d.). However, if he took exercise on land, he also took pleasure afloat.

The small ports and seaside villages of the south coast of Devon had become very fashionable in the early 19th century - Sidmouth in particular, even before the visit in 1819 of the Duke and Duchess of Kent with their daughter, the future Queen Victoria - and the summer regattas of the popular resorts of today were first held at that time. William hired boats (at 3s. or 4s. per outing) on at least fifteen occasions, to witness/participate in boat races not only at Sidmouth, but also at Dawlish and Shaldon. Culturally, there are expenses listed for concert and theatre tickets, a subscription to a music festival and to a library. There is even an intriguing payment in September of 3s. for a conjuror! In addition, William sought to improve his intellectual and social skills, and the *Account* records that he paid for 19 Dancing lessons, 21 Drawing lessons and 22 French lessons.

William's own personal expenses were modest. His washing cost 6s. per week and small amounts were paid to a tailor, linen-draper and boot maker. He bought stockings, night shirts and night caps, but fourteen shirts (costing £1.2s.) were made for him by Martha Cleave and delivered to him in Putney by John Cleave. Clothes were repaired where possible, including a hole burnt into his great coat by a candle (9s.6d.). His only sartorial extravagance appears to have centred on gloves of which he bought seven pairs in the course of the year.

Dowager Lady Molesworth (1761-1842) William's paternal grandmother

Caroline Molesworth (1794-1872) = William's aunt

The three silhouettes were made in 1821 by an artist who signed them with the initials I.O. At that time the Dowager Lady Molesworth & her daughter Caroline were living in London at 14 Hertford Street. William must have been enjoying a stay with his grandmother.

The major payments listed in the *Account* are for fees/salaries/wages and travel. The final draft paid to Mr Carmalt was for £29.12s.7d. but it is not itemised, and it remains unclear whether this charge covered only basic school fees or included extra items. Mr Bartholomew was engaged at a salary of £250 pa - a generous sum for that time - but, like John Cleave he was paid in arrears, so that only one quarter of the tutor's salary (£62.10s.), and only half (£13.2s.6d.) of Cleave's annual wage (£26.5s.) are listed, but William was accountable for payments for lodgings for Mr Bartholomew, and he also paid (£5) for a suit of black clothes and two guineas for a pair of boots for Cleave. The largest single payment was for medical treatment: Dr Lecke and Mr Hardinge (apothecary?) were paid £133.13.8d. in July, and there were further expenses incurred in buying medicines, pills, potions and, intriguingly, 2s. for 'black doses'! It may also be reasonable to conclude that boxes of game and fruit (for which carriage only had to be paid) were part of a recommended diet. Travel expenses were also a major element in the *Account*. William's return journey to school in Putney in January 1824 via Goodamoor and Cobham cost £10.6s.2d. and his contribution of one third of the expenses in travelling to Edinburgh with Bartholomew and Cleave (hiring four horses for the journey of 448 miles) came to £30. William was also charged with payment for Cleave's journeys to and from Putney, and his trips to and from Pencarrow with William's horses.

The above headings make up all but a few pounds of the £408.3s.8d. total amount listed in the *Account*. What has not been mentioned are small, but regular, purchases of items such as pens, stationery and postage, but there is no inkling of what luxuries William may have purchased himself out of his allowance and pocket money. The *Account* ends on a note of mystery. It records a payment of three guineas made when William left Sidmouth to 'old Betsy, your nurse'. Tantalisingly, this is the only occasion she is mentioned and we know nothing about her apart from the fact that the gift (a sizeable amount to give to a family retainer in 1824), clearly indicates considerable affection and gratitude. It may be that it was a parting gift to 'old Betsy' who was to remain at Pencarrow and not travel to Scotland with the family, but it is unlikely that the mystery will ever now be solved. The death of Sir Arscott Ourry Molesworth on 26 December 1823 left his widow, Mary, responsible for the upbringing of the six children of their fourteen-year marriage. The loss of her daughter Caroline, one of twins to whom she had given birth in 1813, who died less than six weeks after her father in February 1824 was another cruel blow, but it served as an added reminder of the care which would be needed to protect the delicate health of her eldest son, William, now the 8th baronet, and it prompted her return to her native Scotland taking him and her other children with her.

George Street, Edinburgh

Published by kind permission of Hamish Horsburgh (www.oldandnewedinburgh.co.uk)

Lady Molesworth took a lease on number 97, George Street which was to be the Molesworth base for the next six years. George Street is a major street in the heart of the eighteenth century 'new town' of Edinburgh, and was an elegant and very desirable residential area of the capital. It was first laid out in 1767 and the development was nearing completion when Lady Molesworth took up residence in 1824.

Once installed, William set about his studies with his, by now, customary remarkable determination and energy as the programme he set himself illustrates:

	Monday	Tuesday	Wednesday	Thursday	Friday	Saturday
a. m.						
6.30-7.30	Botany	Botany	Botany	Botany	Botany	Botany
7.30-9.30	"	"	"	"	"	"
9.30-10						
10-11	German	German	German	German	German	German
11-12	"	"	"	"	"	"
p. m.						
12-1	French	Italian	French	Italian	History	Maths.
1-2	History	Maths.	History	Maths.	"	History
2-3	"	"	"	"	"	"
3-6						
6-7	Geography	Geography	Geography	Geography	Geography	Geography
7-8	Maths.	Maths.	Maths.	Maths.	Maths.	Maths.
8-9	"	"	"	"	"	"
9-10	Laws &	Laws &	Laws &	Laws &	Laws &	Laws &
10-11	"	"	"	"	"	"
Laws & = Laws &c. = Laws, etc.						

At first sight this represents an unrelenting academic grind, but it was a self-imposed regime designed to achieve his driving ambition which was, in his mother's words, to 'satisfy his natural love of study and desire of knowledge.' It is true that he allowed himself breaks of half an hour for breakfast and a further three hours to dine and take a break from study in the afternoons, nevertheless the daily prospect of two hours of studying 'the Laws' and from 9pm-11pm is not one which many young teenagers would relish - especially after eight prior hours of study!

In a letter to his aunt Caroline written in July 1825 he wrote of 'being employed' [in addition to the above curriculum] with Livy, Heroditus, Latin and English themes and translations, Gibbon and Logic. Mr Bartholomew, who had accompanied him, was employed as his principal tutor for William's curriculum in his early days in Edinburgh, but other teachers were engaged. We know, for instance of Dr Gaetano Demarchi, an expatriate from Piedmont, who gave William lessons in Italian and who became his 'guide, philosopher and friend.' By 1826, William was taking advantage of the academic opportunities of being in a university city, visiting the university library and attending lectures given in the faculties which most interested him - Mathematics, Natural Philosophy, Botany and Chemistry.

William was fortunate in two respects. His mother and her family, related as they were to David Hume, knew many of the Edinburgh academics, and William's own industry and intellectual curiosity recommended him to the Edinburgh professors who, according to Lady Molesworth 'took a liking to William and treated him not as a boy, but as an associate.' He was fortunate in the calibre of the professors whose lectures he attended. Sir John Leslie, an eminent mathematician and physicist, held the chair of Natural Philosophy; Thomas Hope was the Professor of Chemistry and a charismatic lecturer, and Robert Jameson was the Regius Professor of Natural History, with a particular interest in geology and mineralogy, and he was the founding editor of the *Edinburgh Philosophical Journal*. Another intellectual and family friend who greatly influenced William was Sir George Sinclair, a fervent advocate of catholic emancipation and the emancipation of slaves - two objectives which were dear to the radical politician that William was to become. All these men were towering academics in their own right and greatly influenced William to hone his analytical reasoning powers in their disciplines, but they also helped to fashion his priorities and values in life. It should be stated that he was not content merely to absorb the theory of the subjects he studied in Edinburgh. He carried out his own experiments whenever possible, at home (where his experiments were not encouraged by his siblings, who did not share his enthusiasm for practical tests), or in a small laboratory which he set up in Portobello, a suburb on the eastern outskirts of Edinburgh where, on one occasion, he nearly died as a result of inhaling chlorine gas.

It must not be thought that William's intellectual curiosity was confined to what his future brother-in-law referred to as the 'exact and natural sciences.' By the age of fifteen, William had laid the foundation of a library by devoting his pocket money to the purchase of 'the sterling and the solid,' in literature and he set about collecting classical works of 'authority and instruction.' He was a voracious but slow reader, but this enabled him to digest and retain what he read, and it was said, for example, that he knew Milton's works by heart by an early age.

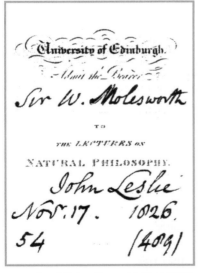

Lest it be thought that William's years in Edinburgh were all work and no play, it is clear from references in letters he wrote in the late 1820s after he left Scotland, that he enjoyed some social life there. He makes it plain that he did not have a high opinion of the young ladies he encountered in Edinburgh society; he thought them 'flirty and giddy', and prone to 'excessive gigling(*sic*) and laughing' two faults which he considered 'approached almost to a crime in young ladies.' We learn little more than the names of the young ladies and nothing about their particular attractions, but, on several occasions when William wrote from Germany during his stay on the continent from 1828-31 in answer to references in letters to him from his sister Elizabeth, he sought confirmation that his 'taste [in members of the opposite sex] is a good one,' and that, given one young lady's popularity, his 'opinion is much followed.' None of the letters to William have survived, and we can only wish we could learn more about a Miss Manners, to whom he sent his love in a letter to his mother shortly after his arrival in Cambridge, a Miss Lamont and the Miss McDonalds, with one of whom he was desperately in love at the same time that he claimed to be in love with Eileen Colquhoun. He disparagingly judged the young female component in the 'noblesse' of Munich 'an ugly set of devils,' and 'society' in the Bavarian capital was sadly lacking the good looks and the vivacity that the Miss McDonalds could provide. He deplored the bad taste of Miss Mitchelson (his 'ci-devant (i.e. former) flame' in marrying an 'old fellow,' implying that she should have done better for herself, and he was not surprised that a relation, Elizabeth Munro, was much admired; he sent her his regards and his regrets that he would not be able to dance with her – 'a loss of little consequence to her, except that I am become tolerably good.'

The only degree of intimacy which is revealed in his correspondence from Germany concerns his cousin Margaret, the daughter of his mother's younger sister Anne's marriage to Alexander Munro. She was two years younger than William, but clearly there was a very affectionate, albeit jocular and innocent bond between them. Shortly after the start of his tour, William asked his sister to give Meg 'two kisses' from him. In a subsequent letter from Munich he wrote: 'Ask my fair cousin Margaret if she still preserves some tender memories of her beloved Billy, or if 1,000 miles has entirely effaced every recollection - this dreadful thought makes me shed a torrent of tears marked by the spots in this letter.' Elizabeth Molesworth obviously complied with this request as, in his next letter to his sister, William wrote; 'I am amused at Meg's candid confession that she would have given me as many kisses as I chose, provided that I had made use of the frequent opportunities to ask for them. Tell her that I am still very faithful.' The diminutives Meg & Billy are obvious indicators of the affectionate familiarity of the relationship between the young cousins - indeed I have come across only one other instance in which William is referred to as Billy, and that was in his mother's diary when she recorded her son's return to Pencarrow from boarding school just before his father's death in December 1823.

Although William attended university lectures and was permitted to use the university library, he was never formally entered as an undergraduate member of Edinburgh University. Whether Lady Molesworth herself considered that her son would benefit from a more conventional and structured course of study, or whether she yielded on this occasion to pressure from her late husband's family to further his education in England, she arranged for William to be admitted in 1827 as a gentleman commoner at St. John's, the Cambridge university college from which both his father and his uncle William had earlier graduated. However, in a letter to his mother within weeks of his arrival, he wrote 'I like Cambridge very much, but I absolutely detest St. John's.' There can be no doubt that William enjoyed the independence away from his family, and he revelled in the opportunities to go hunting almost at will,[4] but it is equally clear that he found the intellectual demands of his university course frustratingly unchallenging, and the college supervision of his studies irksome. He was taken to task by his Tutor, The Revd. Richard Gwatkin, for failing to attend mathematics lectures in which William found his fellow undergraduates 'blundering through propositions in the first book of Euclid,' while he considered that his competence was quite as advanced as that of the lecturers. With time on his hands and apparently little intellectual challenge, he kept up his German lessons and started to learn Spanish.

A quarrel soon developed between William and Gwatkin. The cause of it is not clear and although William later referred to it as 'trifling', it made him quite determined not to stay any longer in a college which was generally considered the worst in the university, and where he had been treated in an 'ungentlemanly manner.' He claimed that 'times have changed since my father and my uncle lived here' and with very few 'acquaintances' in St. John's - he mentioned only Charles Lyne whom he had known in as the son of the Rector of Little Petherick, a Molesworth family living near Pencarrow in Cornwall - he moved as quickly as possible to Trinity College where he maintained he had four times as many 'acquaintances,' including Charles Buller from another Cornish-based family well-known to his uncle, and whom he had also known personally in Edinburgh where Buller was tutored by Thomas Carlyle before he went up to Cambridge.

His move to Trinity was achieved only after some difficulty over payment of the financial penalty imposed by St. John's, but while he was clearly happier to be amongst friends in his new college there is no evidence to prove that it was a move for the better academically. His Tutor in Trinity was Higman (whom Lady Molesworth had met three years before in Sidmouth), and his Dean was Hamilton; his lodgings, with his own furnishings, were out of college and he was looked after there by Duncan McLean, his manservant who had come with him from Edinburgh, and who was to be a constant at his side until William's early death in 1855.

William was destined not to finish his studies and graduate from Cambridge. Another quarrel in which his involvement was initially peripheral led to him being sent down. In the spring of 1828, Edward Duppa, his friend and rescuer after his hunting accident, together with some other students fell foul of the college authorities as a result of the consequences of a quarrel at an unlicensed gambling party, and were sent down from Cambridge. William, no doubt with the memory of his (in his own mind) harsh treatment by his Tutor in St. John's still very much alive, championed Duppa's cause to the extent that he considered himself to have been so insulted by Duppa's Tutor, Henry Barnard, that he felt compelled to challenge him to a duel with pistols. When the affair became public knowledge, the Mayor of Cambridge summoned William and Barnard to appear before him, bound them over to keep the peace for a year and, in the circumstances, Trinity had no option but to expel William. The hope that William's departure from Cambridge, coupled with a year's grace would soften attitudes was not realised, despite an unrealistic and unsuccessful plea from Barnard's aunt to Lady Molesworth to intercede and dissuade her son, the encounter, it will emerge, was merely postponed for a year.

William's time at Cambridge was not a success. He may well have enjoyed his independence, but he did not make the most of his opportunities. This caused his mother 'great painful anxiety.' The anxiety to which she termed his 'short residence' gave rise was principally over the expenses William incurred, but there may well have been concern that her son did not readily accept standards imposed upon him. To be fair to William, Cambridge in the 1820s was a university experimenting with reforms with some of which William may well have been unhappy - particularly in his mathematical studies which were being influenced by new analytical methods - Richard Gwatkin of St. John's was an ardent proponent of the differential notation in calculus. The political sympathies of the university were not to his taste, they were Tory, very Protestant and opposed to Catholic emancipation. The only university lecturers were the professors, not all of them bothered to deliver lectures, leaving the teaching of undergraduates to the college tutors, all bachelors required by statute to be in holy orders, whose teaching sank to the lowest level of the students in their college and was, at best, skimpy, mechanical and limited by their individual capabilities. The custom practised in his uncle's time whereby gentlemen of noble birth were allowed degrees without examination was no longer permitted, a change which would not have concerned William, serious student that he was, but the religious test which had to be passed before proceeding to a degree was still in place and, given the scepticism which he had acquired in Edinburgh, he may have found this unacceptable. Added to which, as he had personally experienced, the discipline to which the undergraduates had to accept was narrow and pettifogging and the college authorities were often tactless and unsympathetic.

William was eighteen years old when he was sent down from Cambridge. He was too old for conventional schooling, he had outgrown personal tutors. He had shown a reluctance to accept university disciplines. For all his individual efforts and application, his education was incomplete. Lady Molesworth resolved to follow an accepted pattern of the time to send William on a purposeful tour of the continent. She sought advice from her friends in Edinburgh and decided to send him first to Germany where some of her acquaintances had sent their sons. She was much concerned about his companion/guardian/mentor on the tour and settled, with William's genuine enthusiasm, on Sir Joseph Straton, a family friend of longstanding.

Sir Joseph Straton had started life as Joseph Muter, born in 1777, the youngest son of Colonel William Muter and his wife Janet, née Straton. He joined the army as a Cornet in the 2nd Dragoon Guards in 1794 and, after having fought in three campaigns in the 13th Dragoons in the Peninsular Wars 1810-13, by 1815 he had risen not only to command the 6th Dragoon Guards in the battle of Waterloo, but he also assumed command of the brigade of which his regiment belonged upon the death in action of the brigade commander, Sir William Ponsonby. Towards the close of the battle Muter was wounded, but he had distinguished himself in the action to the extent that his conduct was recognised and rewarded with the Waterloo Medal, his appointment as a Companion of the Order of the Bath, a Knight Commander in the Guelphic Order of Hanover and the award of the Order of St. Vladimir of Russia (4th class). Inheriting his mother's family estate in Kincardineshire, Scotland, on the death of an aunt in 1816, he changed his surname to Straton. He was promoted to the rank of Major-General in 1825, Lieutenant-General in 1838 and to the Colonelship of the 8th (Inniskilling) Dragoons in 1839. He died in London on 23 October 1840.

At the beginning of August 1828 William, accompanied by Straton, set off on a tour of the continent which lasted, with a break in the summer of

1829, until he returned to England in March 1831 in time to celebrate the anniversary of his majority two months later. He visited Italy from the late autumn 1829 until early 1831, but the principal aim of the initial months of the tour was for him to acquire fluency in the German language while, at the same time, continuing to develop the social attributes so essential in a young man of his rank.

William crossed from Dover to Ostend by steam packet on 3 August 1828, spent a month at Spa before travelling via Aachen (at the time Aix-la-Chapelle), Cologne, along the banks of the Rhine to Coblenz, and thence to Offenbach, a small town close to Frankfurt-am-Main, where he arrived at the end of September. Here he lodged 'en pension' for two months with the family of a Dr Becker, and quickly and readily adopted a profitable routine. He usually took his meals with the family - he breakfasted at 7.30am, dined at 3pm, drank tea at 7pm - but he was not enamoured of the German cuisine (too many sausages and vegetables and not enough meat, but he did like the quality of the regional Hock wines and their price, 3d per bottle!). Consequently, on occasions his servant, Duncan McLean, cooked him some 'English comforts' on a pan of charcoal or a spirit lamp in his rooms. He described his 'apartments' in the Becker household as small, and his sitting-room as an 'extraordinary melange' of objects forming a 'perfect chaos in which all attempts to create order only render disorder more evident.' He devoted the morning to his studies, first completing his German exercise (translating *The Vicar of Wakefield*), then having his German lesson with Dr Becker who corrected his exercise and listened to him reading German. Before dinner, he found time to do some rifle-shooting (on one occasion he claimed to have hit five bulls at one hundred yards) and fencing, and he then spent the afternoon and early evening in the 'Collegium' (club), where he played billiards, chess, read the papers and smoked. He returned to the Beckers for tea and then read philosophy until 'Somnus sheds his poppies on my eyelids.' Interestingly, in the light of his later professed agnosticism, he wrote to Elizabeth from Offenbach to say that there were no Anglican churches there and, since he considered himself 'too much attached to my own religion,' he had resolved not to attend any 'foreign service.' It is impossible to know whether he intended Elizabeth to accept this statement at face value or, being close to her brother, she was expected to appreciate its irony.

William remained a pensioner of Dr Becker for two months. He formed a high opinion of the doctor and considered him 'very clever', but was not so impressed with Frau Becker, who 'thought herself clever too,' but wasn't; moreover, William thought her 'old and not good-looking.' Nevertheless he recommended that his fourteen year old brother Arscott should follow in his footsteps 'for a year or two'. It would not prove expensive - £100pa for board and instruction with an additional £50 living allowance. It was never intended, however, that William's own stay in Offenbach would be for more that eight weeks, at the end of which, he set off for Munich where he arrived on 20 November via Heidelberg, Stuttgart and Augsburg - not the most direct route, but more picturesque. Here he found himself no longer under the wing of General Straton (who had been forced to return at the beginning of October to attend to urgent business at home), but of Lord Erskine, the British Minister at the Bavarian Court. David Erskine, 2nd Baron Erskine, in gratitude for the kindness he had received in Edinburgh at the hands of William's mother's family, and because of a family connection with them through his aunt, Mrs Erskine, undertook to take responsibility for William during his stay in Munich. In a letter to Lord Erskine written in January, 1829, Lady Molesworth stated that she had 'mighty reasons for wishing him [William] to remain abroad for a year or two' and she was prepared to allow him 'sufficient income to defray his expenses and support his rank in life.' The Minister offered him an apartment in his own house but, perhaps with his Offenbach experience fresh in his mind, William declined the offer and found lodgings of his own, but he saw the Erskines every day and frequently dined with the family.

Lady Molesworth had been heartened by reports of her son at the start of his tour. In Spa his conduct was described by General Straton as 'steady, proper and gentlemanlike...he evinced no turn for any species of dissipation.' His regime at Offenbach was very much study-orientated and, no sooner had he arrived in Munich, than he had engaged masters to improve his dancing, drawing, and fencing. He also engaged tutors to improve his grasp of German (which he could now 'read with facility, but it does not yet flow with ease from my tongue') and French, the language of choice in society in Munich. He described his usual day as starting with dancing at 8am, and a morning of study finishing at 1pm; then to the Erskines to ride with them (there were six daughters in the family), or to escort Lady Erskine to the shops or on a promenade; dine with the Erskines at about 5pm, then three times a week to the theatre, return to drink tea with the family before returning to his lodgings and being in bed by 11.30pm.

Lord & Lady Erskine gave William the entrée into Munich society and he took full advantage. He was presented at Court wearing (as instructed by Erskine) 'regimentals', though quite what uniform the eighteen year old was entitled to wear is unfathomable. He described the King, Ludwig I, as a 'good-natured person' who talked 'equally ill to everyone in their own language', but he does not think highly of Munich society in general: 'except for a few English and a Frenchman there is not a companionable being here.' He was not impressed by the women whom he labelled a 'd - d ugly set of old devils.' In his opinion there were not more than two pretty persons among the noblesse, but he considered married women much more pleasant than Misses, whom he found gave themselves airs and were flighty and shallow. He was above all disappointed that (except by the bourgeoisie) French and not German was the language spoken in society, and that his fellow compatriots (or 'the other animals of my nation' as he referred to them) never initiated conversations with the Germans in their own language, nor danced with them unless they were obliged to do so.

Within a month of William's arrival in Munich the carnival season opened, although he does not admit it, the social demands on his time and energy must have had some adverse affects on his studies, which he no longer mentions in his letters. He gives an exhausting description of his activities in this season, and gives an indication of why to the society ladies in Munich a good dancer was 'looked upon as a Deity' and a bad dancer was 'esteemed amongst the d - d.' It appears that William was out almost every night attending balls which started at 7pm or 8pm and lasted for at least seven hours. The programme consisted usually of eight waltzes, three 'galopes - a dance unknown in England and most dreadfully tiring' - three quadrilles or other dances, and ending with a cotillion which usually lasted for an hour! But there were also 'pick-nick' sledge parties which started from the city in the early afternoon, then going out into the country before returning in the evening by torchlight. William gained quite a reputation as a reckless sledge driver, but the liveries of his outriders - light-blue, white and silver, white breeches and jockey caps with silver tassels - were constantly 'excessively admired.' The most exotic of these parties was given by the Queen, Therese, when thirty sledges assembled at court at 1.30pm, then were driven five miles to a royal castle where all the guests had a splendid dinner and about four hours of dancing before driving back to Munich in their sledges each preceded by two flambeaux. William was pleased with the informality at these dances where there was no need of an introduction to a young lady before inviting her to dance because the rank and status of all those attending had been vetted as being 'comme il faut.'

The carnival season ended in mid-March with a splendid royal ball at which lasted from 6pm to 5am. Those invited were given characters from a popular comedy, and had to march through the rooms in procession according to one of the scenes in the play. William went as Don Juan in a Spanish costume, and the public 'chose to affirm that I had the most splendid costume in the room,' but he paid a price for his nether regions were clad not in breeches, but only in silk 'drawers', and he caught a cold.

Munich began to pall on William after the carnival. He wrote everyone 'is going or has gone,' and he had had his fill of the cold winter climate. In April, he wrote to his mother that he thought she had spent long enough in Edinburgh and that 'it would be a considerable advantage to my sisters to pass a few years in a foreign country.' He suggested that she might like to spend the Christmas of 1829 in Italy, where he had thoughts of joining her and of 'keeping house together,' where the warm climate would be more agreeable to him. He suggested that Lady Molesworth should come with his sisters and his ten-year old brother, Francis, who would derive great benefit from 'early acquiring foreign tongues,' moreover a tutor for Francis would act as a companion for William himself. His other brother, fifteen year old Arscott, would stay behind with his tutors but would, in time, move to Offenbach following in William's footsteps to stay with Dr. Becker.

But it was not only the weather or the 'ennui' from which William was suffering in post-carnival Munich which was making him impatient to leave Bavaria, he had to keep his word and attend to the unfinished business of the challenge he had issued to Henry Barnard the year before. It had been agreed that the duel would take place on 1 May 1829 in Calais, and in mid-April William and McLean set out to travel the 700 or more miles from Munich to Calais to honour his obligations. They took nearly a fortnight to travel the distance, but arrived in time. William was met in Calais by Henry Leach, the family solicitor, having been sent across the channel expressly by Lady Molesworth to look after William's interests and perhaps act as his second. Of the duel itself, there is no account other than the rather laconic comment by William in a letter to his mother from London dated 2 May, 1829: 'I am happy to inform you that I am alive and well. I could not hit my adversary, do all I could.' Barnard was, clearly, no more successful with his pistol, but honour had been saved on both sides. Nevertheless, Lady Molesworth must have been greatly relieved, and will, undoubtedly have echoed the wishes of the Marquess of Queensberry who wrote to her shortly after he learned the outcome of the duel 'I hope, for your sake, that he will be a good Boy for the future.'

William's movements in the summer of 1829 are not clear. In early May he wrote to his mother from Stephen's Hotel in London to say that he was 'infernally tired of travelling all alone,' and that he intended to stay in England until she, or General Straton, would travel abroad with him. He also stated his intention to visit Devon to see his solicitor and pay a visit to his uncle William who was Rector of Beaworthy, as well as being Rector of two livings in Cornwall (St. Breock and St. Ervan). There is, however, no record of what William did in the next few months while he was in England, but from a letter he wrote in December 1829, it is clear that his mother, his two sisters, Elizabeth (aged eighteen) and Mary (aged thirteen), together with his eleven-year old younger brother, Francis, had not accompanied him to the continent, but had followed shortly afterwards in his footsteps to Italy. His other brother Arscott (aged sixteen) remained behind in Edinburgh to be tutored for entrance to Oriel College, Oxford.

His letter, dated 23 December 1829, was addressed to his mother in Florence, where Lady Molesworth and his siblings had arrived earlier that month, shortly before William's departure from that city to Rome. He was pleased that his mother, like him, had found Florence 'so agreeable,' but he did not attempt to hide the fact that, for him, 'the eternal city' (Rome) held the greater attraction. There is a subtle change in the contents of William's letters in the second part of his continental tour. There are still references to the serious study characteristic of his youthful years, but there is now a greater emphasis on the enjoyment of his social life and his 'chief occupation - sight seeing.' His enjoyment of 'society' in Germany had been limited by the fact that he had come across too few kindred spirits, whereas, in Italy, it appears that he found a thriving circle of foreign nationals, mostly English, who were, like him, seeking to learn and take pleasure in the traditions, history and culture offered by Rome and Italy.

It is evident from the names on the invitation to William, his mother and his sister, Elizabeth, (Mary had not yet 'come out' and so was ineligible and Francis was far too young) to the ball given by the bachelors in Florence at the end of December 1829, that they were a cosmopolitan group. Of the thirty-five aristocratic hosts, sixteen were British and nineteen foreign, mostly Russian and German. In Rome, however, William seems to have associated very much in a British circle of society to judge from the names of the hosts at a Ball in the Palazzo Sinibaldi in February 1830, at which: 'no unmarried Lady or Gentleman [will be] received out of fancy dress.' All the forty 'Bachelors at Home' on that occasion were British, of whom Francis Stapleton, later 7th baronet, and Messrs. Binning and Jardine had followed William from Florence, together with James Colquhoun, the brother of the fondly remembered Miss Colquhoun of Edinburgh. There were others in Rome whom William mentions who were known to Lady Molesworth and her family - Mrs. Greenwood; the Scott family who were 'as kind as usual and offer to take me everywhere' and whose son, the Revd. George, was a particular friend of William; Lady Macdonald Lockhart and her younger son who William thought was 'the most agreeable young man I know'; Thomas Buchan-Hepburn, later 3rd baronet; Geordie Leith; Sir James Mordaunt; Sir H. Trelawny; Mr & Mrs Carpenter and the Hon. John Dundas, a son of the 1St Baron Dundas.

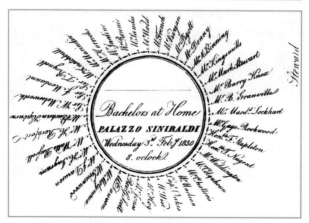

With his friends Marindin and Stapleton he hired a set of rooms in the Corso 'the best situation in Rome' - four bedrooms, 4 sitting-rooms, and servants' rooms for 22 Louis per month, and his carriage, horses and coachman cost him a further £22 per month. He goes sight seeing for about two hours every day initially but, not surprisingly soon establishes a routine although he seems regularly to have attended 'gay, very gay parties' most nights: 'to bed at 3, rise again at 9, then drawing or fencing — in drawing I am very diligent and am making progress; then to breakfast and so to Arabia, my master with a long beard is from Caldea(sic)[5]. None of my masters can speak any language but their own. 12-2 sometimes Italian or receive visitors; at 2 my carriage to pay visits or promenade; return to perform my lessons, dine at 6 (dinner for four about 7/-), then from 9 until 3 to evening parties and my rooms are open to my friends for smoking.'

At the end of January 1830, William wrote to his mother that he was 'more & more pleased with Rome,' he urged her to come to join him in time for the carnival, due to start in mid-February at the climax of which in the last week 'the city goes mad.' He offered to book rooms for her and his siblings in Baldi's Hotel, but advised that the best seats for viewing would be in his rooms where, she should be reassured, they had invited many ladies. He offered a further incentive to Elizabeth to come, by telling her that she would be able to join the many ladies who rode every day. He further whetted their appetite by telling them of a pre-carnival fancy dress ball which he and James Colquhoun were to attend, William in the costume of Ivanhoe, Colquhoun as Robin Hood. As for himself, much as he was looking forward to the carnival, he was also looking beyond it to the Spring when he hoped to engage a painting master and to go with him to draw from nature in the 'environs' of Rome which he thought were splendid.

In 1845, William presented his wife, Andalusia, with a leather bound volume of sketches he had made while he was in Rome and Naples in 1830. The location of the sketches is usually provided, but the dates are often omitted. However, the date on a sketch of the San Benedetto Monastery in Subiaco confirms that although he was still in Rome at the end of April, by mid-August the dates and subject matter of is sketches show that he had moved to the Bay of Naples.[6]

Only two letters written by William from Naples survive. In the first, dated 24 August 1830, we read that it was the intention of Lady Molesworth, having followed in her son's footsteps from Florence to Rome now to travel (with her family and a companion, Mrs Macoun) to join William at Castellamare on the bay to the south of Naples. William described his lodgings there as 'very pleasant,' but as he described, they had provided him with stimuli, intellectual and emotional. He wrote of a fellow lodger, a Roman Catholic priest 'who was intent on [turning] me Catholic: you know how strong I am in religion, though a little puzzled what doctrine to support. I, however, stood my ground as a good protestant leaving him highly edified at my pious sentiments and only pitied me for not allowing the supremacy of the Pope. There was also a very pretty nun in the lodgings who was 'deeply grieved at my state of damnation, though I rue more deeply the wounds inflicted by her black eyes on my tender heart. Such a confession to the chaste spouse of Christ, I suppose, would in her opinion increase my torment in the next world — or perhaps *au contraire*.'

It is highly unlikely that the prospect of sharing lodgings with two such proselytizers would have deterred someone of Lady Molesworth's faith and mettle from journeying to Castellamare, but we learn from William's last, undated letter from Naples that she did not join her eldest son, but she did send Francis to spend some time with his older brother. William wrote of his plan to take Francis on an excursion to Sorrento and Amalfi before sending him back to Rome to rejoin his mother and sisters but, for the first time, William also gave an indication that his thoughts were turning homewards. He had also read newspapers and had had news of political events in England, particularly of the Tory party's grudging approval of Catholic emancipation and of the then Prime Minister, the Duke of Wellington's firm opposition to parliamentary reform. His friend, John Dundas, had returned from Italy to stand in the general election in September and had been elected to serve as the member for Richmond. As William later explained to

Francis Alexander Molesworth at Naples in 1830

Elizabeth Molesworth 1829

Harriet Grote, 'my friends conjured me to return, representing in forceful language the obligation I lay under of joining the Liberal cause at so critical a juncture and the chance of me carrying an election as member for Cornwall if I were on the spot.'

This sense of duty and his burgeoning radical opinions will also have been prompted by the political atmosphere in Italy. William had learned of the earlier (1821) nationalist revolt in Piedmont from Gaetano Demarchi, his Italian tutor in Edinburgh, who had been a leading light in the unsuccessful revolt. Now, nearly ten years later, following the success of the July 1830 Revolution in France, he was aware of the threat posed to the established order in Italy and in Naples in particular, by the 'carbonari' - a secret society dedicated to the cause of freedom, independence and constitutional government. This resurgence of revolutionary feelings in favour of a unified Italy resulted in initially successful and relatively bloodless coups in the Papal States and the northern Italian states of Parma and Modena through which William passed on his journey home.

We do not know when Lady Molesworth arrived in Naples, or whether she joined William before he set out for England, but she was there when he wrote to her from Bologna in January 1831 in which he described his journey north from Naples. It took him 30 hours by carriage to Rome and a further non-stop journey of 3 days and nights to reach Bologna. He went on:

'You will be surprised to hear that an intended revolution has broken out here & at Modena, & extended itself over Romagna as far as Rimini & then likewise to Parma & Piacenza. We were very much surprised to see the tricolor cockade. Nothing can be more quiet & peaceable &, except the nuisance of having our passports read every 10 or 12 miles & had to get down from our carriage once or twice to go & see the Deputies, we got on without trouble. There has not been a dozen of men killed, except in Modena where some canon has been fired. Where it will end, it would be difficult to say & would not be without torrents of blood. For myself, I found it amusing &, though detained, I went into caffes(*sic*) & laughed & talked to the people.'

Lady Molesworth was still in Naples when William wrote his next letter to her from Lyons, dated 13 February 1831. The remainder of his journey through northern Italy by way of Parma, Piacenza and Turin was made in bad weather, but 'everywhere we were received with the greatest politeness and all the information they could give.' He crossed into France by the pass of Mont Cenis - an experience which he found was hair-raising: the ascent and descent were both difficult and dangerous; the narrow road was covered in deep, soft snow and William's carriage had to be dismounted and placed on a sledge, but he surprised himself in that he found that he could 'nod off on the edge of a precipice, as well as on a bed of down.'

28

On his arrival in France he was told by the custom house officials that England was now a friend of France and he was made welcome there and elsewhere in his journey through France. He merely stayed overnight in Lyons before pressing on to Paris, where he spent the next five weeks. The weather was, in his words 'damnable,' as a consequence he did little sightseeing, but he bought an 'immense number of books and made acquaintance with several *savants*.' He learned of Lady Molesworth's plans to return home and thoroughly approved of her intention not to follow his route overland in Italy, but to go instead from Naples by steam to Marseilles and he recommended, when she broke her journey in Paris, that she, too, should stay in the Hotel de Breteuil - he had found it one of the best and cheaper than lodgings. By the 19 March in a letter from Paris, he confessed that he was 'infernally tired of this place & commence to be desirous of reaching home.' He left the French capital the next day, travelling via Rouen and Calais before experiencing a 'tempestuous 12 hour crossing' of the Channel. He then continued to London for a reunion with his grandmother and aunt at Cobham, before reaching at Pencarrow on 5 April 1831, just six weeks before he attained his majority and became officially eligible to stand for parliament.

Notes & References

1   Sir Henry Raeburn's portrait of Sir Arscott Ourry Molesworth hangs in the Inner Hall.
2   Oakley Brighton was the gamekeeper at Pencarrow.
3   John Cleave served as William's manservant until Duncan McLean took his place c.1828.
4   William's health was never robust, but he was a keen, almost fanatical, follower of the hunt. In November, 1827, when following the Earl of Fitzwilliam's hounds, he fell & broke his collar-bone but, with the help of a fellow undergraduate (Edward Duppa), he remounted & rode for a further 50 miles before returning to Cambridge to have the bone set! He wrote to his mother begging her to provide him with good hunters for 'not to ride [at Cambridge] is out of the question.'
5   For Caldea read Chaldea. William was studying Semitic languages in contemplation of a future tour of the Middle East.
6   It had been hoped that a manuscript journal in the Pencarrow archive of a classical tour of Naples & its environs would shed further light on William's 1830 itinerary. However close scrutiny has revealed that, although the journal was contemporaneous & mentioned Lady Molesworth, William was not the author.

SIR WILLIAM MOLESWORTH, BART.

LADY MOLESWORTH
(ANDALUSIA GRANT WEST NÉE CARSTAIRS)

Two watercolours painted by Sir William Molesworth during his 'Grand Tour' in Italy in 1830/31

Sir William Molesworth and the Foundation of the Wadebridge Farmers' Club

The new theories, inventions and practices at the heart of the Industrial Revolution at the turn of the nineteenth century affected all commercial undertakings, and farming was not exempt. There was concern and disquiet about a number of issues - the consequences of the enclosures of common land, the fluctuating corn prices, the varying length of tenancy agreements, the gradual shortening of the terms for hiring labourers, the reluctance of landlords to invest in farming infrastructure (especially buildings, drainage and fencing), the introduction of horse-powered agricultural machinery, all of which combined to lead to the formation of Farmers' Clubs/Associations throughout England. It was hoped that landowners would come together with farmers to share new ideas and aim to create a more harmonious, prosperous, mutually beneficial relationship between tenant farmers, yeomen farmers and landowners.

By the 1830s, there was growing concern in Cornwall that farming was in a parlous state: the land was of very variable quality; there were granite uplands, heavy clays, free-draining loams and although the climate was usually benign, a Board of Agriculture review in 1817 concluded that 'Cornwall comprises a greater proportion of inarable lands than any other English county.' At that time, with less than 10 per cent of the population involved in agriculture, there was no place for farming in the traditional county toast, 'Fish, tin & copper.' Nevertheless, there was a growing determination among farmers in the Duchy that all avenues to a more dependable, productive and prosperous future in agriculture should be explored. To that end, Farmers' Clubs were formed. As elsewhere in the country, the members were principally yeomen, tenant farmers with landowners and local gentry welcomed as honorary members. However, to quote the President of the Probus Club in 1843: 'these gentlemen [the hon. members] are not expected to attend at the monthly meetings, as such practice might prevent that free and useful exchange of sentiments which ought to prevail, freedom of thought and speech during the discussions being particularly desirable, but they might attend at anniversary dinners. They might also assist by donations of books to shew that they, the landlords, take an interest in the welfare & improvement of their tenants.' It was also hoped that: 'intelligent agricultural friends will freely come forward with the results of their local, practical & observational knowledge, either as public lecturers or as instructive periodical conversational contributors.'

According to reports published in the *West Briton*, a number of clubs were founded in the late 1830s or early 1840s. There are references in 1838 to monthly meetings in Penryn to coincide with the cattle market; farmers' clubs were active in Probus (which had amassed a library of more than 300 books by 1846), Veryan and Callington (with an annual subscription fee of five shillings for ordinary members) by the following year. In the 1840s, other club meetings were reported in St. Columb (1841), St. Germans (1841), Illogan (1841), St. Austell (1842) and Launceston (1846). This list is not comprehensive, but the purpose of this paper is to give an account of the composition, conduct and concerns of the early years of the Wadebridge Farmers' Club (henceforth WFC) founded by Sir William Molesworth, Bart.

A letter dated 11 December, 1841, addressed to 'Sir Wm. Hooker at the Royal Botanic Gardens, Kew, has come to light in the archive of the Director. It was written by Thomas Corbett, the head gardener at Pencarrow, in his capacity as the WFC secretary. In the letter, he claimed that the Wadebridge Farmers' Club was 'the largest and most influential society for the diffusion of agricultural knowledge in Cornwall,' implying that it had been in existence for some time. We know that the first club dinner was held in 1841, but there is some evidence to suggest that Corbett's claim may not have been too boastful.

Sir William was not a practical farmer (even Trescowe, his home farm at Pencarrow, was leased) but, in the immediate surrounds of Wadebridge, he was the landlord of farms in the parishes of Egloshayle, St. Breock, St. Mabyn, St.Kew, St. Minver, St.Tudy, and through the steward of his estates (Thomas Woollcombe, a Devonport solicitor) and his local agent (John Lakeman, who farmed a small farm on the Pencarrow estate at Costislost), he encouraged many of his tenants to become members of the WFC.

Evidence of Sir William's interest in and support for the farming industry can be seen in his subscription to the East Cornwall Agricultural Association / Launceston Agricultural Society (£2 pa from as early as 1832), but particularly in the prize (plate/silver cup to the value of £5) which he offered annually from 1837 to promote turnip husbandry in the Wadebridge area - this would suggest that a club or association of farmers was already in existence by that date. Further evidence of his interest in farming was his attempt in 1831 to get Woollcombe to influence his Pencarrow tenant farmers to adopt new farming practices when their leases came up for renewal when he attained his majority. The attempt was not an unqualified success initially but, as Woollcombe reflected many years later in 1857, the methods advocated in 1831 had been universally adopted by then by WFC members. Woollcombe, himself, had further encouraged agricultural improvements by subscribing £3.10s. annually for a prize to be awarded to the WFC member adjudged to have grown the best crop of grasses. Sir William's interest in the aims of the WFC persisted into the 1850s, when he presented the club with £25 to promote the cultivation of flax, in 1855, shortly before he died, he donated £25 towards the cost of the purchase of a 'reaping machine' for use by the members.

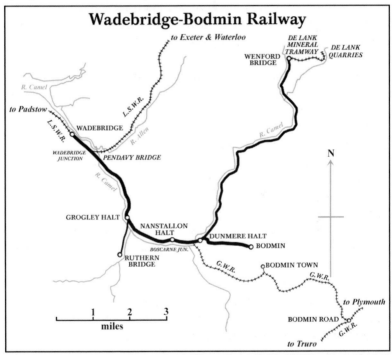

However, perhaps the most telling sign of Sir William's early interest in farms and farming is illustrated by his initiative in the development of the Wadebridge-Wenford Bridge railway, which was intended, initially, only to carry freight. The freight was sea-sand from the Camel estuary and it was Sir William's idea to carry it to fertilise unproductive farmland in the Camel valley with the aim, as he put it, 'to make two blades of good grass grow where one blade of poor grass grew before.' In 1831, the year in which he attained his majority, he commissioned at his own expense, a civil engineer from Plymouth to suggest and survey a route for a main line railway between Wadebridge & Wenford Bridge with branch lines from Dunmere to Bodmin and from Grogley to Ruthernbridge. The engineer reported in January 1832, and the route was approved. In May, the Bodmin & Wadebridge Rail Company was incorporated with authority to raise capital of £22,500, with shares priced at £25.[1] In July, the company directors were appointed (with Sir William as Chairman) and work began. Construction took eighteen months, the final cost totalled £35,000, or £2,450 per mile, it was only the fourth railway to have been built in this country. In addition to paying for the survey, Sir William was the principal shareholder (65 shares costing £1,625); he donated land free of charge for sections of the railway where it passed over his land; he financed the dredging of the river Camel, the building of wharves by the railway at Bradford's Quay in Wadebridge, and he invested a further £3,258.16s.6d. before 1840. The line was finally officially opened in September 1834. Although it soon carried passengers as a matter of course and also other freight (much to the annoyance of local carters), throughout Sir William's life, it continued to fulfil its primary function and deliver the sand inland to Wenford Bridge.

Press coverage of the Farmers' Club meetings was almost exclusively limited to the anniversary gatherings. The unreported monthly meetings of some clubs (as in Penryn) are known to have coincided with the local cattle market day, but it was not until 1856 that the WFC decided to follow suit. There are incidental, imprecise references to WFC meetings, including a lecture on manure by Gregory Brabyn, a Wadebridge merchant, in January 1846, but the anniversary meetings were first reported in December 1847 and December 1848. In subsequent years the anniversary meeting was held in January, almost invariably on the second Tuesday of the month. Attendance numbers (including 'strangers from a distance') fluctuated according to the weather, there were never fewer than thirty but, in 1859, as many as seventy attending the event. The members met at the *Molesworth Arms*, dined at 3pm. in the long room on 'good & bountiful fare' provided by the landlady, Mrs Charlotte Hicks. After the meal, the cloth was removed, the loyal toast was proposed and discussions about farming matters took place, liberally interspersed with many other toasts.

A list of the membership of the WFC in its early years is appended (Appendix A), together with a map of the farms known to have been associated with the WFC (Appendix B), but they are far from being comprehensive, since they have been compiled solely from the published accounts of the anniversary meetings, they include only the names of those who spoke, featured in the annual competitions, participated in one of the toasts, or whose farm is mentioned. The ordinary membership included gentlemen farmers (e.g. Hoblyn of Colquite and Stephens of Trewornan), yeomen farmers (e.g. the Pollards of Bodieve and Clapper), tenant farmers; there were also a number of honorary members. Club arrangements were in the hands of a committee, it was managed according to a set of rules which, if broken by ordinary members, attracted fines or penalties from which honorary members were exempt. Subscriptions were 10s. for ordinary members and 1 guinea for honorary members. At the annual anniversary dinner, the toasts, most of which involved a wordy proposal and an equally verbose reply, were many: The Queen (on occasions, other members of the royal family); the Clergy; the Army & Navy; local MPs; the Ladies; the Royal Agricultural Society; the President/Patron; the Chairman; the Town & Trade of Wadebridge; Visitors/Strangers; Representatives of other Farming Clubs; the Officers of the WFC; the Press; the Judges of the Club Competitions and, of course, the Competitors (with spokesmen for both winners & losers).

Published by kind permission of Peter Tuthill

Molesworth Arms (19th Century)

37

The topics discussed at the anniversary reunions of the WFC reflected very much the concerns of the mid-nineteenth century agricultural industry mentioned above. Members were urged 'to speak their minds, but express their sentiments with good humour and propriety, and to prevent anything disagreeable, they should refrain from party or personal allusions.' Politics were not forbidden by the rules of the club but, for a number of years, there was a tacit understanding that political opinions were not to be aired. However, after the repeal of the Corn Laws and the increasingly regular presence at the annual reunion of the local members of parliament, this custom lapsed; the range of debate was not thereafter even tacitly politically circumscribed. There was never quite the confrontational 'them & us' (landlord & tenant) debate characteristic of some Farmers' Clubs, partly because, although Sir William attracted some criticism for not attending meetings after 1843 when he presided over the reunion, the members appreciated his financial support, his tenants defended him as being a good and understanding landlord. He had abated the rents of his farms by 10% in the depression of the mid-1830s, again reduced the rents by 10% on the repeal of the Corn Laws in 1846 and at about the same time, he made the game on his farms the property of his tenants. There were concerns expressed in general about the lack of landlord investment in the infrastructure of their farms - poor drainage, inadequate storage buildings, lack of secure fencing - but the limited accounts which have survived show that Sir William spent approximately £1,000 per year on repairs and new buildings on his Pencarrow farms from 1831-41. The accounts for 1848 show repairs & new building work was carried out on twelve farms, the 1849 estimate for repairs & new buildings amounted to £1,734.12s. This included drainage ditches, sinking wells, water channels, the conversion of outbuild-ings, as well repairs to the farmhouse at Treveigan and the erection of a new 'dwelling house' at Tredruston. In 1852, further expense of £625 was incurred for repairs, enclosing the farm yard and building a new cattle linhay, at Hay farm in the same year, £560 was spent on building on to the dwelling house, levelling the farm yard and making a pond. The work undertaken or proposed shows no indication of crisis management, but rather a planned, realistic, forward-looking approach.

Among other topics discussed was the length of farm leases, the general consensus was that a lease of twenty-one years (rather than one of seven or fourteen years which was not uncommon in Cornwall), would give the best returns against the capital investment of both the tenant and the landlord. In 1850, the demise of the small farm was envisaged and deplored by one speaker, who predicted that it would lead to the introduction of the 'bothy' system, whereby the unmarried farm workers instead of 'being boarded in the master's house, sitting at his table, receiving all that attention that both as regards their health, their moral and religious training which servants ought to receive, are huddled together in lofts and out-houses, where they are entirely free from restraint and admonition.' In 1852, Thomas Olver of Trescowe, a regular contributor to the anniversary discussions on a great variety of topics, expressed deep concern about the education of farmers' children. Young 'farmers-to-be' he argued, should be taught in schools 'where they would be taught the rudiments of the various sciences connected with agriculture, and have opportunities of seeing and assisting in farm management of the most approved character.' His plea for such a school was not answered in Cornwall, although some Agricultural Schools were established elsewhere in the country at that time. The various merits of dung, sand, bone dust and Peruvian guano as manure were debated. It was accepted that each had its use, but the efficacy of each depended principally upon the type of soil on which it was spread. There were also discussions about the relative usefulness and cost-effectiveness of the working horse versus the ox, the view taken was that there was a balance in favour of the horse, the pros and cons of the modern agricultural imple-ments, from improved designs of ploughs, scarifiers, turnip and manure drills, horse-hoes to water-driven and steam-powered threshing machines, reaping machines were debated.[2] But the recurrent topics for discussion concerned crops (white and green), cropping and grasses.

The white crops most generally cultivated were wheat, barley, oats, and the green crops grown as animal fodder were principally turnips and mangolds/mangel-wurzels, but cabbages and carrots were also planted. Attempts were made to introduce other crops — potatoes, rape and some vetches — but not to any great or widespread effect. Good husbandry had long dictated the need to rotate crops in order to extract the greatest yield and at the same time, increase the fertility of the soil, but there was much discussion among WFC members with regard to the best rotational system of cropping. Some argued in favour of a wheat crop followed by turnips or another green crop, then by barley or oats before being laid down to pasture for two or three years: others favoured wheat followed by (1) barley, (2) turnips, (3) barley or oats, (4) grass for three years. The dangers of forcing the soil to produce yields without allowing it sufficient time to rest and recover fertility was often stressed, but it was a temptation for tenant farmers on a short (7 year) lease or in the final years of a longer lease when the tenant's lease was unlikely to be renewed. There was discussion about the best method of sowing seed (whether broadcast or drilled) best suited to the cultivation of the loamy soil of the parishes of Egloshayle, St. Tudy and St. Mabyn, in contrast to the more clayey soil of St. Kew, St. Enodoc and St. Minver.

All were agreed on the importance of having good grass on a farm, both as pasture and to provide a hay crop, but there was no consensus about what constituted the best seeds to sow. Thomas Corbett, the head gardener at Pencarrow, the first secretary of the WFC was instructed by his fellow members to seek the advice and cooperation of the Director of the Royal Botanic Gardens at Kew in an attempt to arrive at the best mixture. In Corbett the WFC had a man well qualified to make this inquiry. Since 1830, Corbett had been a full Fellow of the Linnean Society, the society pre-eminently concerned with the promotion of the study of all aspects of the biological sciences. The principal sponsors for his election included Thomas Bell, Professor of Zoology at London University, John Claudius Loudon, a leading botanist, garden magazine editor, and significantly in this instance, George Sinclair, to whom he refers in his letter (*see page 161*). Sinclair was the gardener/horticulturist who had supervised experiments to compare the performance of different species, various mixtures of grasses and herbs on different types of soil which had taken place from 1809-1816 on the Duke of Bedford's Woburn estate. There is no record of Sir James Hooker's reply to Corbett's inquiry, but we do know that Corbett (credited in 1846 by W.F.Karkeek, the author of a *Report on the Farming of Cornwall* with having paid more attention to the growth of grasses than any other person in Cornwall), had his own recipe which he recommended not only to his fellow members in Wadebridge, but also to other Farmers' clubs in the county. We also know that the mixture of seeds which he advocated - rye grass, cocksfoot grass, rough-stalked meadow grass, red clover, with additional white clover and trefoil to be added if the land was to remain in pasture for longer than three years - did not find universal favour. The mixture was tried by several of the Wadebridge farmers but, in 1845, it was generally found to have produced a heavier and coarser sward than was ideal, the debate continued - so, too, did Corbett's preoccupation with the challenge. In a letter written in 1844 to his son, William, who had emigrated to New Zealand two years previously, he refers to clover and grass seeds which he has sent to Sir William Molesworth's younger brother, Francis, in New Zealand, William Corbett's employer. He wrote that the 'seeds [must] be sown separately on very clean ground to get the seeds from each pure', and added 'I should like to know how the different clovers and grasses do with you, I will send more seeds of any that does well.'

From the outset, in common with all other farming clubs in the county, competition between members was encouraged with the aim establishing the best practices. Competition categories were established, rules laid down in an annual attempt to identify the best overall farms and farmers, also those who were adjudged to have produced the best green crop and the best grass crop of the year.[3] There was no compulsion among members to enter the competitions, some members obviously entered only when they considered that they had a chance of winning, but there were a number of members, principally gentlemen and yeomen farmers who participated each year.

It is unfortunate that no records of the WFC have survived and that newspaper reports of its activities did not appear until 1847, the year before Thomas Corbett died at the age of fifty. He was not mentioned in the 1847 report, but we know, by deduction, that he had been succeeded/replaced as the secretary by 1844 by William Pollard of Clapper. The gardens at Pencarrow as they are today are as much a lasting tribute to the skill and abilities of Corbett the gardener, as they are of Sir William Molesworth the designer, but it is puzzling that the WFC did not even mention his death at their reunion meeting and dinner in 1848, only four months after his death, particularly since much of the post-dinner discussion involved a debate about the optimum mixture of grass seeds. Corbett was a knowledgeable, self-made man; with little or no formal schooling; he had educated himself to the extent of being worthy of election as a Fellow of the Linnean Society; he was capable of delivering a detailed ex tempore lecture lasting two hours on the Physiology of Plants, and he had been cited as a reliable authority in the 1846 official report on farming in Cornwall. Why did he become the forgotten man? Was it because he came from 'out of county,' and that his Northumberland/Yorkshire background was held against him - there were several reports that some WFC members resented farm bailiffs/agents who were not Cornish? Were his opinions unpopular because they were based too much on science and theory, and not enough on experience and farming practice, or was it simply because he was the only member of the club who was a paid employee, who was not directly involved in any aspect of farming? It is unlikely that the puzzle will ever be solved.

The annual reports on the state of the WFC were usually encouragingly optimistic but in 1851 the agricultural depression led to a dip in its fortunes. Interest had fallen away to the extent that the monthly meetings were suspended; there were only three entrants for the prize for the best managed farm, none of them was a tenant farmer; some members had resigned and even Thomas Olver of Trescowe was sufficiently downhearted by the full effect of the repeal of the Corn Laws then being felt and by the uncertain political state of the country that he, too, was tempted to stop his subscription. By 1854, however, prices to farmers had recovered, there was an increase in the number of entrants for the farming competitions, the largest number yet (nearly 100) attended the WFC anniversary dinner. It is, perhaps worthy of note that, for the first time, the two local members of parliament for East Cornwall were present, and that, again for the first time, political solutions to problems in the agricultural industry were unrestrainedly debated, and were to be a feature of the anniversary gatherings in the following years.

Sir William Molesworth died in October 1855. He had not attended the WFC anniversary meetings since he had taken the chair in 1843 but, although he had incurred some criticism for his non-attendance, it is clear from the annual reports that most members recognised that the WFC meetings were, of necessity, low down in the pecking order of his responsibilities as an MP and cabinet minister. He was recognised as a good and fair landlord, and gratitude for his support was expressed at all the anniversary gatherings where his interest was represented each year by the presence of his local agent, John Lakeman of Costislost, and by the fact that his solicitor, steward of the Pencarrow estate even took the chair on one occasion. Tributes were paid to Sir William for having 'conferred a great benefit on the neighbourhood by founding the Farmers' Club, and for being its greatest supporter.' At the meeting held in January 1856, Thomas Olver, the tenant of the Pencarrow home farm, paid a personal tribute to Sir William, saying that, even though he did not share his political opinions, he had never had an unpleasant word from him, nor had he attempted to persuade him to give him, his landlord, his vote. He had found Sir William to be exactly what he purported to be - 'a liberal-minded man, liberal in word and deed.'

The link between the WFC and the Molesworth family was not severed by the death of Sir William. He was succeeded as patron for the next thirty-three years by his widow, Andalusia, who, much to the relief of the members, pledged to maintain the same level of financial support as her husband had given. She, in turn, was succeeded as patron by Sir William's widowed sister, Mary Ford, who was even more generous in her support until her death in 1910, although the etiquette of the day precluded the presence of either Andalusia or Mary at the club's anniversary meeting. The last of the Molesworth baronets, Sir Lewis, although he continued to live at his mother's family home at Trewarthenick, and never came to live at Pencarrow, was nevertheless elected patron for the last two years of his life, 1910-12, at which point the Molesworth connection was finally severed. However, the only participating member of the Molesworth family in the WFC was the 9th baronet, Sir Hugh, the cousin who succeeded Sir William. He did not occupy the family seat at Pencarrow but, as the Rector of St. Petroc Minor at Little Petherick, he not only lived locally, but he also actively farmed the 50 acres of his glebe. Sir Hugh attended only one anniversary dinner in his cousin's lifetime, but attended from 1858 - 1861 and occupied the chair in 1859.

When the Royal Agricultural Society of England was founded in 1839, a prominent reformer said: 'If our farmers will inquire what is done by the foremost of them, they will themselves write a book of agricultural improvement on the broad page of England.' - It is surely praiseworthy that the Wadebridge Farmers' Club contributed substantially to the chapter on Cornwall.

Notes & References
1   £1 in the 1830s is the equivalent of £50 in today's money.
2   Some of the machinery which will have been discussed is illustrated in App. C.
3   For details of the competitions, see Appendix D.

Appendix A

Membership President/ Patron - Sir William Molesworth: (1841-55).

Hon. Members (Gentry and Local Worthies): Thomas Agar-Robartes MP (Lanhydrock); Gregory Brabyn (Merchant, Wadebridge); Edmund Hambly,(Solicitor, Wadebridge); Francis J. Hext, (Tremeer, *Chairman 1855*); Capt. William Hext RN [½ pay], JP (Tredethy); D. Peter Hoblyn, JP (Colquite, 300; Nicholas Kendall MP (Pelynt); Revd. Sir Hugh Molesworth (Little Petherick, 48); Edmund Norway (Timber merchant, Wadebridge); William K. Norway (Solicitor; Wadebridge); Edward Stephens, JP (Trewornan, 226, St. Minver, *Chairman 1847-54*); Trehane Tickell (Surgeon, Wadebridge); T. Wills (Merchant, Wadebridge); Morrish Wilton (Gent. Egloshayle); Thomas Woollcombe (Steward of the Molesworth Estates).

Visitors: Mr. T. Allanson (St.Columb); John Bassett Collins (Attorney, Bodmin, & Sec. Bodmin & Trigg Agricul. Soc.); John Bryant (Merchant, Padstow); Thomas Clarice (Chemist, Bodmin); F. Enys Esq.; Nicholas Grose (Tremadart, 320, Duloe [born St. Kew]); Capt. Horndon (D. of C. Rifle Rangers); Mr. F.J. Hunt (Army); Thomas Martyn, (Merchant, Allin Cottage, Egloshayle); Mr. Physick; Ensign R. Pollard; Mr. Rickard (Representing Thomas Woolcombe, Devonport); Lt. Stephens, RN.; Sampson Tresawna (President, Probus FC); John Wills (Farmer, South Petherwin).

Clergy: Rvds:
Dr Joseph Benson (St Breock); John Ellis (St Minver); N. Every (St Kew); E. Green (St Breock); George Hext (Tredethy); C. Hosken (Luxulyan); John H. Rendall (Treneglos); W.H. Smith (St Minver); George Somerset (St Mabyn); Edward Shuttleworth (Egloshayle); J. Wilkinson (Lanteglos).

Ordinary Members *(Names of farms, location and acreage given where known):* James Bennett (Trevinnick, 150, St Kew); Charles Broad (Washaway); James Carter;Thomas Cleave (Trelill, 314, St. Breock); Thomas Corbett (Pencarrow, Head Gardener); John Davey (Egloshayle, *Vice-Chairman 1853*); Richard Fradd (Bodieve, 72, Egloshayle); John Greenwood (Washaway, 50); Richard Grose, (Hendra, 303, St. Kew); Mark Guy (Roscarrock, 698, Endellion); Abraham Hambly (Treblithick, 135, St Mabyn); F. Hambly (Wadebridge); Charles Hicks (Pengenna, 150, St. Kew); John Hocken (Hustyn, 90, St. Breock); William Hocken (Trenarlett, 300, St.Tudy); John Hooper (Trequites, 120, St Mabyn); James Jeffery (Lower Bodiniel, 160, Bodmin); Hart Key (Pawton, 600, St. Breock); John Lakeman [Costislost]); Thomas Liddell (Treglines, 320, St. Minver); Samuel Martyn (Egloshayle); Charles Menhenick (Middle Amble, 750, St. Kew); John Menhennick, (Burnire, 390, Egloshayle); William Menhenick (Treraven, 180, St. Breock, *Treasurer 1854 -5*); Thomas Olver (Trescowe, 690, St. Mabyn); Edmond Pollard (Egloshayle Road, 130); Richard Pollard (Bodieve, 300) *{son of William P, Sec 1848 - }*; William J. Pollard (*Sec. -1846*), [then {from 1849} Henry Pollard] (Egloshayle); Richard Rouse (Trelawder, 166, St. Minver); Thomas Sobey (Rook, 400, St. Kew); Henry Symons (Roserrow, 700, St. Minver); Henry Vercoe (Pendavey, 364, *Treasurer 1841-53*); C.Vigars; James West (Hay, 110, St. Breock); William West (Higher Croan, 170, [200 '61]).

Press Reporters: Henry Hooper (*West Briton*); Mr. Chomley (*Cornwall Gazette*).

Appendix B

Farms associated with the Wadebridge Farmers' Club

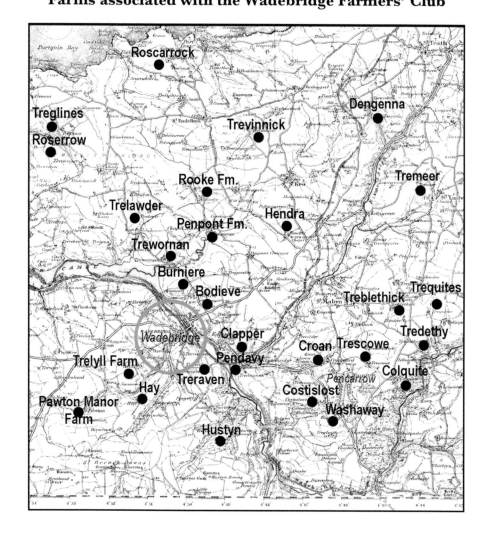

Appendix C

Early 19th Century Farm Machinery

1. Bell's Reaping Machine

2. Garrett's Portable Thrasher
(as packed for Travelling)

3. Common English Waggon

4. Kirkwood's Grubber

(Images 1-4 taken from Morton's 'Cyclopaedia of Agriculture' c.1856)

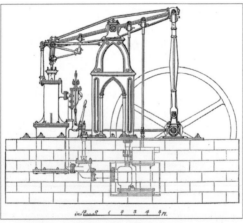

5. Sims of Redruth 6hp steam engine

(Taken from an illustration in W.F.Karkeek's *Report on the Farming of Cornwall*, 1846. The engine's purpose was to thresh corn, but it was also designed to be adapted to 'shake straw, winnow & bruise grain, chaff straw, grind malt, oil-cake & bones.' It could also be adapted to cook fodder for horses, cattle & pigs by steaming turnips, potatoes & chadd. The cost, £180-200 proved too much for any member of the WFC.)

Appendix D
Competitions

With the aim of achieving higher standards and getting a better yield from their farms, members were encouraged to compete against each other and allow their farms to be judged annually according to clearly established criteria. Although the winners and the comments of the judges were made public at the annual dinner, the complete list of competing farms was never published. From comments reported, however, it is clear that not every member opted in to the competitions, and those who did, did not do so every year. The judges were recruited from within the membership, and the farms were usually classified as 1st class (farms of more than 100 acres), or 2nd class (farms of less than 100 acres although, in the early years, this category was subdivided into a 3rd class for farms of more than 5 but less than 25 acres. In the 1840s, the competing farms were inspected in June, August and December but, by 1854, the inspection seems to have taken place only in November.

The most prestigious award, for the best managed farm, went to the farmer who earned the most points (marked from 1 [poor] to 6 [very good]) in the following categories common to all sizes of farms:

1. The extent of the green crop [grasses, vetches, vegetables] in proportion to the land in tillage for corn.
2. Whether the farm is clear of weeds.
3. The management and application of manure.
4. The state of the fences.
5. The quantity, nature and quality (breed and general condition) of the live stock.
6. The utility of the agricultural implements and machinery on the farm.
7. The standard of the general crop of all descriptions (considering the nature and quality of the land).
8. General improvements which have been made [since the last inspection].

Curiously, a penalty of 2-4 points (1st class farms) and 1-3 points (2nd class farms) was deducted from the total gained by entrants who farmed their own land & were not 'rack-renter' farmers. The winner of this competition for 1st class farms was awarded 'handsome piece of plate' to the value of £10, and the runner-up received plate valued at £5. The winner among the 2nd class farms received a silver cup to the value of £4, and the runner-up £2.

In addition to the competition for the best farm overall, there were competitions in both classes for the best green crop and for the best grass crop with points ranging once again from 1-6 being awarded in each category . The points for the green crop were awarded as follows:

1. The orderly drilling of the crop.
2. The cleanliness and good order of the land.
3. The quantity of land under green crop in proportion to white crop.
4. The best crop in proportion to the quality of the land. The first class farms competed for the Molesworth Cup, a silver cup valued at 5gns, and the runner-up received £1. In the 2nd class competition, the winner received £2 and the runner-up 15 shillings. In judging the grass crops points were awarded for:

1. The greatest quantity in proportion to the size of the tillaged land.
2. The cleanliness of the land.
3. The best crop, hay or pasture, in proportion to the value of the land.
4. The surface of the ground to be well covered.

In this competition the winner in the first class was awarded the Woollcombe Cup, a silver cup valued at £3.10s, and the runner-up received £1. In the second class competition the winner received £1.10s; the runner-up earned 10 shillings.

Pencarrow 1908

The Right Hon. Sir Wm. Molesworth, Bart., M.P. (1810-1855)
Secretary of State for the Colonies. The Strenuous and Successful Advocate of a
Liberal Colonial Policy
Presented to the Canadian Parliament by his sister, Mary Ford, of Pencarrow, Cornwall, 1898

48

Mary Ford (née Molesworth)

Mary Ford (née Molesworth)
1859

Mary Molesworth, the fifth child of the marriage of Sir Arscott Ourry Molesworth, 7th baronet of Pencarrow, and his wife Mary, née Brown, was born in January 1816, and was baptised on 25th January of that month in the church of the Holy Cross on the Molesworth estate at Tetcott, north Devon. In the thirteen years after he came of age in 1811 until his untimely death in 1824, Sir Arscott and his family probably spent more time at Tetcott than they did at the principal seat of the family, Pencarrow, primarily because it provided better hunting country for Sir Arscott but, for Mary, there was nowhere to rival the attractions of the mansion and gardens of Pencarrow, to which she remained passionately attach-ed throughout her long life.

The one person in her family whose affection for Pencarrow exceeded Mary's was her eldest brother, William, who succeeded to the baronetcy at the age of fourteen. Mary was very dose to William and extremely proud of his achievements in politics where, before his early death in 1855, he had achieved cabinet rank as Secretary of State for the Colonies. Mary was also very supportive of all William's initiatives at Pencarrow, particularly his innovative designs for the gardens which he introduced in the twenty years or so after attaining his majority in 1831. It is therefore not surprising that while William, in his will, made his widow the tenant for life of Pencarrow; he stipulated that it should then pass to Mary for her lifetime. The terms of William's will effectively divorced the baronetcy from the family seat for more than fifty years. Andalusia, William's wife, outlived her husband by thirty-three years, and Mary was the tenant of Pencarrow only from 1888 until her death in 1910.

Unlike her brother William, Mary did not keep a diary. We have to rely upon letters to her, from her and about her, some original, some copied,

49

which have survived in the Pencarrow archive, together with occasional contemporary newspaper accounts to provide the details of the picture describing her long life.

The Molesworths, despite showing a talent for marrying long-living wives, did not have a history of living to a ripe old age themselves. Of the first ten baronets, only the 2nd, Sir John (1635-1723), exceeded his biblical allotment of years, and five died before the age of forty-five, yet the wives of the 5th, 6th, 7th and 8th baronets were aged eighty-six, eighty-one, ninety-seven and seventy-nine respectively when they died. In Mary's own immediate family, she lost her father in December 1823 at the age of thirty-four and, six weeks later her sister Catherine died aged nine. Elizabeth, her remaining sister died aged twenty-four in 1836, and her brothers, Arscott and Francis, both died in their twenties, Arscott aged twenty-nine in 1842, and Francis aged twenty-eight in 1846. Her eldest brother, William, the 8th baronet, never enjoyed good health and he, too, died young at the age of forty-five in 1855. Mary, however, had inherited her mother's genes. Mary Brown, born in 1789 and descended on the distaff side from the Hume family of Edinburgh, married Sir Arscott Ourry Molesworth in 1810 and did not die until 1877, outliving her husband by more than fifty years; Mary herself was ninety-four years old when she died in March 1910, having also outlived her husband by more than fifty years.

Mary's life can be conveniently divided into five chapters: first, her childhood until the death of her sister Elizabeth in 1836; from 1836 until her own marriage in 1851; her married years 1851-58; the period waiting to come into possession of Pencarrow in 1888 and finally, her twenty-two years as chatelaine of Pencarrow and the Molesworth estates.

Mary's earliest years were mainly spent in Cornwall and Devon, but after she lost in quick succession both her husband and one of her daughters in the winter of 1823-4, Mary's mother returned with her children to her native city of Edinburgh where, as a consequence of the Hume family connections they enjoyed both a good social life and a stimulating company. William, after attending some classes in the University of Edinburgh, went on to a frustrating and abortive year as an undergraduate in Cambridge University before embarking in 1828 on a continental tour which lasted, with a break in the summer of 1829, until he returned to England in 1831 in time to celebrate his attaining his majority in May of that year. The first part of his tour was spent in Germany, and William's correspondence from that period is principally with his mother, but there are some letters addressed to his sister, Elizabeth. Of Mary, then aged twelve, there is no mention in any of his letters from Germany but, only half in jest, William makes it clear that he has a poor opinion of adolescent girls, writing that even those like Elizabeth on the verge of coming out into society at the age of eighteen, are still too childish and too 'giggly' and 'giddy'. A few years later, his jaundiced opinion of the fair sex had not improved. In the spring of 1844, on moving in to a house in Lowndes Square newly painted on the outside, but rather dirty inside, he wrote to Mary that it 'resembled so many of the female sex, fair without, but foul within.' He must have undergone a damascene conversion before his marriage to Andalusia Temple West less than three months later!

After a summer in England, William returned to resume his continental tour in Italy, but on this occasion he persuaded his mother to visit Italy too, bringing with her Elizabeth, Mary and Francis (Arscott was destined to follow in his brother's footsteps by furthering his education in Germany). It appears that mother and siblings did not join William for any length of time, but rather did their own tour, usually following in his footsteps from Florence to Rome and then to Naples. Mary's reaction to the Italian experience is nowhere recorded, but it undoubtedly will have allowed her to appreciate and share William's enthusiasm for Italian gardens and, subsequently, wholeheartedly endorse his gardening innovations at Pencarrow.

Before, during and after his continental tour, and during his life in London as a bachelor, William was a dutiful son and wrote regularly to his mother, but his sister Elizabeth was the sibling with whom he felt most in sympathy, and with whom he corresponded from time to time. Partly to get over her death in May 1836, William took his mother and Mary on a trip to see Francis in Frankfurt, moving on 'en famille' to visit Prague before returning to England via Berlin and Hamburg. It was after this trip that William turned to Mary to write of his social life in London, to describe the political scene and to share his enthusiasm for plants and nurseries. Not many of William's letters to her have survived and, strangely, given her lifelong ambition to preserve for posterity anything relating to her brother, none of her letters to him. William's letters are usually addressed to 'My dear Mary, and invariably end 'Your affectionate brother, William', but he also addresses his sister as 'My dear wise Dot', and 'Mol. My Love.' The content of the letters varies from a serious, if rather biased and intolerant review of politicians and the political scene of the day, to ribbing her about one of her 'admirers', Charles Austin, the lawyer who gave the monkey puzzle tree its name at Pencarrow, principal amongst them, but when Mary and her mother are on a visit to Edinburgh in January 1838 he wrote that he supposed that her 'lots of admirers [may] have driven the barrister from her mind.' He wrote amusingly about his social life exaggerating his gallant and flirtatious behaviour at London parties and, bearing in mind his opinion that females are great gossips, he chides her at the end of one early letter containing a banal account of his day to day activities, to 'impart in strict confidence and eternal secrecy the contents of this letter to my Mother, to Elizabeth, to Miss Dietz, to Tommy etc., he might as well have written 'Uncle Tom Cobley and all! In the same vein, he concludes another letter 'I am what I am, and the 'what' is your affectionate brother, William Molesworth.'

But it is to Mary, above all, that he wrote about gardens and plants. He described the plantings at Pencarrow, commenting on their success or failure. He wrote about visits to nurseries and waxed lyrical about a visit to Loddige's nursery in Hackney in 1843 which filled him with 'envy and desire of possession', for 'all the riches, all the vegetable pride of the tropics was there collected....It was indeed a new world.....On one plant alone, about fifteen feet high, we calculated there were in full flower two thousand of the most beautiful camellias.' His letters often accompanied specimens sent from Pencarrow to his sister in London, or from London to Pencarrow when she is in residence there. In 1844, he goes out of his way to procure for Mary an 'Order for Admission' to the Horticultural Gardens at Chiswick.

That Mary's good opinion was something very much desired by William emerges clearly from his letters to her in 1844 when he returned to London society, after nearly three years out of politics, living at Pencarrow where he was preoccupied with his plants and with work on his edition of the works of the seventeenth century philosopher Thomas Hobbes. William left Pencarrow a bachelor in March 1844, but when he returned four months later, he was on his honeymoon, having married Andalusia Grant West, a widow, on 9 July at St. George's, Hanover Square. It is not known how, where or exactly when William met Mrs West, but he will have known that London's *beau monde* would consider that he had made an unwise attachment. Andalusia's parentage was unknown, she had no fortune, she had studied music with a view to a professional career, and there was even a strong rumour that she had appeared on stage at Drury Lane. However, as far as William was concerned, she had the great advantage of having no parent or guardian to place the religious or political objections to his agnosticism and his radical, reforming principles which had scuppered his chances of marrying Julia Carew in the mid-1830s, then Caroline Trelawny a few years later. Nevertheless, if he was to be sure of her acceptance by society, he had to win over his mother, and he set out to do so by gaining

Mary's support.

Mary and her mother arrived in London in April, not staying with William in Lowndes Square, but taking a house in Chester Street. William, with unaccustomed vivacity and geniality, did his best to ingratiate himself with his mother and her friends on the social scene. He wrote to Mary extolling the charms of Andalusia, he persuaded his mother and sister to 'chaperone' outings with Andalusia to dances, the theatre, the opera; Mary even accompanied William and Andalusia on a visit to the Botanical gardens in Regent's Park. Mary was convinced that her brother was seriously in love and at the beginning of June she gave a party at which Mrs West sang 'well' according to William, who remarked that there were 'plenty of nice, some superior, people.... many pretty girls and women to adorn the rooms'. Four days later he proposed to Andalusia, who promptly accepted. The date of the wedding was fixed for exactly a month ahead, even though William did not meet Andalusia's parents until some days after he had proposed.

While William and Andalusia were honeymooning in Cornwall, Mary undertook to supervise the transfer of Andalusia's possessions to William's Lowndes Square house, and also to overlook the changes and redecoration necessary to turn the bachelor accommodation into a home for the married

Richard Ford 1840

couple. When William and his wife returned to London, the Dowager Lady Molesworth and Mary went down to Pencarrow to pack up their personal belongings, both mother and daughter returned to Pencarrow occasionally after William's marriage, but never *'en famille'*; they were invited to stay after the season or over Christmas as guests in a house party. Until William's death, Mary continued to socialize with her brother and sister-in-law, even going to Brighton for short break with them both in 1847, but inevitably she became increasingly involved with the London circle of friends and acquaintances of her husband, Richard Ford, after her marriage in 1851, when, also, her West Country retreat moved from Pencarrow to Heavitree House, her husband's property near Exeter. Richard Ford lavished quite as much enthusiasm on Heavitree as William had on Pencarrow. Like his brother-in-law, Ford carried out building alterations and additions; he also planted pines and cypresses and he designed beautiful grounds, terraces, gardens and borders, but this time in the Moorish style and not the Italian. Mary had found a kindred spirit.

Mary was thirty-five years of age when she married, her husband was twenty years older, twice a widower, intellectually distinguished, but of a much more conservative nature politically than her radically-minded brother.

John Gendall. View of Heavitree House and Gardens c.1822.

Once again we do not know what brought the pair together, or when their first meeting took place, but they may well have become acquainted through Mary's literary interests. Richard Ford was a regular contributor of articles and reviews to the *Quarterly Review*, a journal politically sympathetic to the Tory aims of preserving the *status quo*, which had been established principally to counter the influence of the *Edinburgh Review*, the Whig-supporting periodical which, ironically, was regular reading for Sir William Molesworth. Towards the end of her life, Mary claimed to have read every number of the Quarterly for the previous sixty years, but it must be presumed, given her loyal support for her brother, that her interest in the periodical was primarily literary not political.

The first known contact between Mary and Richard Ford occurred in May 1850, when he sent Mary the autographs of the Bishop of Exeter and George Borrow for the collection she was known to be making. Little over a year later, they were married, like William Molesworth, at St. George's, Hanover Square, making their London home in Ford's house, 123 Park

Street. At the time of the marriage, Richard Ford had three children surviving from his first marriage, and one daughter from his second marriage. Mary was made welcome by all the Ford family, but became particularly close to Clare (then aged twenty-three), the son of his first marriage, who was to have a distinguished career as a diplomat, and a daughter Henrietta (aged eleven), known affectionately as Meta to whom she became a second mother. Ford writing to Mary's mother two months after the wedding gives a flavour of their early married life: 'We rub on pleasantly and much enjoy the repose of London 'out of town'. We vary existence by suburban trips of an approved cockney and connubial character One day we steam down to Greenwich, champagne and whitebait; another, we float down the beautiful Thames at Twickenham, to the disturbance of swans and punters.' Then, in August 1851, the Fords went on a protracted honeymoon tour to the north of England and Scotland, all the while 'junketing as friskily as Lord Palmerston,' as Ford wrote in a letter. They passed through Malvern where Jane, the wife of Thomas Carlyle, the historian, described 'Ford's last new wife' as 'a decidedly clever looking person, whom I could get to like'.

Richard Ford was much occupied in writing articles, reviews and in producing a revised edition of his celebrated *Handbook for Spain*. His health was suffering, but there was, nevertheless, a good deal of entertaining and much socializing in London and Devon where Ford claimed they 'ruralised & rusticated', but Devon was not without its social occasions and excitements. Writing to his mother-in-law from Saltram in November 1854, Ford described how their coach had turned over as Mary and he were returning from a ball in Plymouth - neither Richard nor Mary were hurt, but Mary 'had to walk above a mile in satin shoes and her diamonds'. Earlier in the same year a guest described a party held in London by the Fords: 'No. 123 was a little beehive swarming with drones - upstairs and downstairs - looking at pretty things, eating strawberries and drinking champagne'. She found Ford 'infinitely amusing' and Mary 'a very plain, clever person'.

Mary suffered two calamitous losses in the 1850s. Only two months after entering the cabinet as Colonial Secretary, her brother's poor health finally gave way and he died in October 1855. Three years later, her husband of only seven years died of Bright's disease in August 1858. By the terms of Richard Ford's will, Heavitree House was left to his son, Clare, but Mary continued to enjoy the lease of their Park Street house in London and, as her correspondence with her stepson confirms, she remained a cherished member Ford family. However, her brother's death, or rather the manner of it, caused a rift between the Molesworth family and Andalusia.

Mary, and possibly her mother, held Andalusia responsible on two counts for William's early death: firstly for her unrelenting ambition to become a leading society hostess which made no allowance for the stress and strain to which William was exposed by his life in politics: secondly because of the apparent disregard she showed for the known poor state of her husband's health, to the extent of not calling his doctor to attend him in his last illness until it was too late. Some attempt at reconciliation took place shortly after William's death when Mary's mother, entertained Andalusia when the new baronet Sir Hugh Molesworth and his wife dined with her in January 1857; Mary, her mother and her husband paid her a brief visit when Andalusia was staying in a 'lodging house' in Brighton during her period of mourning, but it did not last. Although William left Mary an annuity of £1,000, Pencarrow was to be Andalusia's for her lifetime. In the circumstances, aware that Andalusia's ambitions to succeed as a society hostess would make her very much London-based, Mary must have found this galling.

It is true that for a number of years after William's death, Andalusia went to Cornwall after the London season, and attracted many leading members of the *beau monde* to her house parties at Pencarrow but, as she grew older, her visits became less frequent and she went more often abroad, to Paris. Mary's social life also flourished, but not in quite the same circle, since she entertained predominantly people associated with the *Quarterly*, well-known and respected in the world of art and letters, but she also valued the friendship of a soldier and military writer, the Bodmin-born Sir Edward Hamley. She followed closely the diplomatic career of her stepson who became Sir Clare Ford, a Privy Councillor and ambassador successively to Madrid, Constantinople and Rome. She felt his death in 1899 and the death of Meta some months later very keenly.

Andalusia became ill in 1886. It was thought by John Vanning the family solicitor, that she was unlikely to recover. At his suggestion Mary, who confessed that it had been seventeen years since she had last spoken to Andalusia, agreed to visit the invalid. A tearful reunion took place; Andalusia recovered, and at least one further meeting took place before Andalusia once again fell ill and died in May 1888. Pencarrow was, at last, to pass into Mary's hands although, small legacies apart, no Molesworth inherited any of Andalusia's personal wealth, property or possessions.

Mary had waited patiently for more than thirty years to take over the tenancy of Pencarrow. For Andalusia, a visit to Pencarrow was characteristically planned to further her social ambitions and, as such, was little more than an extension of the season, but in a rural setting. For Mary it was a joyous homecoming - not only to the house and gardens she loved, but also to 'her people', the estate tenants, employees, the local tradesmen and inhabitants. Mary kept up her lease in Park Street, but spent several months each year at Pencarrow. Less than three months after Andalusia's death, Mary, her wait over, set out for Cornwall to return to her 'father's home.'

Mary described her return in a letter to her stepson, Clare, writing that her long journey by train was 'full of sad memories', but when she got off the train at Bodmin on 14 August, the evening was 'moderately clear" and she drove to Pencarrow in an open carriage. She continued:

'As I drove through Bodmin it seemed to me as if the whole town had turned out of doors, so full were the streets of people all staring at the solitary old lady dressed in deep mourning. On, on I sped and when I neared the Lodges, the road was lined with vehicles of all sizes, shapes and forms filled with people who all saluted me. There was literally an army of men on foot and on horseback. They did not stop the carriage, but all took off their hats - and so far all well and I breathed freely at having so easily got off. On reaching Pencarrow I was given a tremendous cheer and I went out and curtseyed and thanked them warmly for the kindness of their reception. By this time I was fairly done and glad to get to my room and bed. Pencarrow is a Princely possession and requires a princely income to keep it up. I have been over the gardens this morning and walked about the grounds. The trees are in splendid leaf, and those I left small have grown into almost fine forest trees - What a paradise William has created and how little he ever dreamt that the last survivor of his family would now be in possession and writing this record to you.'

Almost immediately Mary set about perpetuating the 'paradise' she had inherited and began a programme of replacing and replanting shrubs and trees, which she maintained for the next twenty years, enhancing William's legacy with an extensive and exciting planting scheme of her own, specialising in conifers. This specialisation, together with William's now mature arboretum originally planted in the 1840s, earned her the Royal Horticultural Society's Knightian Silver Medal for her collection of cones in 1891. Her principal source of supply was Veitch's nursery in Chelsea, but some plants and seeds were obtained from the estates of friends in Cornwall. She supplied *Araucaria* seeds to the biology department of the University of Toronto and, in return, was sent some American elms, sugar maples and Manitoba maple trees. Clare Ford sent seeds of exotic plants which he had come across in the various postings in his diplomatic career, and one of his protégés sent seeds from Japan. In 1908, she was approached by the Royal Botanic Gardens at Kew to carry out a trial planting of the *Rhammus Purshianas* tree to discover whether it would adapt to the climate of the south west It is greatly to her credit and that of head gardener, Aubrey Bartlett, that articles published in gardening journals at the turn of the twentieth century confirm that the gardens and trees of Pencarrow were once again attracting attention for all the right reasons.

Shortly after her arrival at Pencarrow, Mary gave a dinner to her Pencarrow tenantry at which 'there was a large attendance, and a very enjoyable afternoon was passed,' and she wrote to Clare of a dinner given to her tenantry at Tetcott at which there were 103 people present, after which, in the evening she gave supper to the tradesmen and workmen. She became involved with local organisations: she became the patron of the Wadebridge Farmers Club; she gave prizes for the best horses, cattle, sheep and pigs in the Wadebridge and District Agricultural and Cottage Garden Association's annual exhibitions; for the town of Wadebridge, she provided the site and £1,500 towards the cost of the cattle market in 1898; she opened a new scheme for piped water in the town in 1900, and she donated the site of Coronation Park to mark the coronation of Edward VII in

Mary Ford in old age (?)

1902. In these and other ways she identified herself with the life of the locality and, as her obituary recorded 'she was ever-generous when approached for support for a worthy cause, and many of 'her people' had reason to be grateful for generosity and her many acts of kindness.

Apart from a portrait of her aged forty-three painted by Da Monte in 1859, we have no likeness of her, although a photograph which has recently come to light, may well be of Mary Ford in old age. In her lifetime, tributes were paid to her intelligence, her sound judgement, her vitality and her remarkable memory, and to the fact that she had 'the sweetest and most fascinating speaking voice', but no-one remarked that she was a beauty. That mattered little to her, and not a jot to those who knew her. One of 'her people' who attended the tenantry dinner at Tetcott was moved to record his impression in verse. It may be more McGonagall than Wordsworth, but this excerpt speaks from the heart:

We will show Mrs Ford how she's respected by we.
From the Molesworth Family this Lady descends,
And through her we Tenants have found a kind friend.
May her life be a long one, and happy may she be,
To continue the Landlady over those that I see.

In her will Mary Ford expressed the wish for her burial in the churchyard at St. Conan's on Pencarrow land at Washaway, to be a simple walking funeral 'that I may be carried to my grave by my retainers who are Gardeners, Gamekeepers, Carpenters and Weedmen on the Pencarrow estates not exceeding thirty in number.' The *Bodmin Guardian* reported that her wishes were carried out on Tuesday 8 March, when 'a muffled peal was rung on the bells of Egloshayle church, and all over the district blinds were drawn as a silent tribute to the memory of one, who by her innumerable gracious and benevolent acts had rendered happier the lives of those around her.'

WADEBRIDGE,

June 28th 1898

Dear Sir,

Wadebridge New Cattle Market.

We have pleasure in informimg you that the above will be opened on JULY 12th. for general business.

at 11 a.m.

Mrs. Ford, of Pencarrow

will perform the opening ceremony and an Address will be presented to her

at 1 o'clock.

❋ A PUBLIC DINNER ❋

will be held at the Molesworth Hotel.

Chair to be taken by J. J. H. VENNING, Esq.

THE COMMITTEE HOPE TO BE FAVOURED WITH YOUR COMPANY.

CHARLES MENHINICK, Chairman of Committee.

Sir St. Aubyn Hender and
Lady Ingeborg Molesworth-St. Aubyn

When Sir Lewis Molesworth, the last of the Molesworth baronets died on 29 May 1912, the Pencarrow baronetcy devolved upon another branch of the family in the person of the Revd. St. Aubyn Hender Molesworth-St.Aubyn, known as Sir Hender Molesworth-St. Aubyn after he succeeded as the 12th baronet. He was the grandson of the Revd. John Molesworth (1763-1811), son of Sir John Molesworth 5th Bt. by his second wife Barbara St. Aubyn. As a direct consequence of this union, and the subsequent marriage of her niece to the 6th baronet's younger brother, John, when Sir John St. Aubyn died without leaving a legitimate heir in 1839 the St. Aubyn family estate at Clowance (which had been in the family for thirty generations since the 14th century) was inherited by the 12th baronet's uncle, the Revd. John Molesworth. In recognition of his inheritance, he was authorised by Royal Licence in that same year to assume the surname of St. Aubyn after that of Molesworth. After John's death in 1844, Clowance was inherited by his brother, the Revd. Hender Molesworth (the 12th baronet's father, who also adopted the additional St. Aubyn surname by Royal Licence), and the estate passed to his son on his death in December 1867.

St. Aubyn Hender Molesworth-St. Aubyn was born at Portreath on 27 December 1833, and was educated at Helston Grammar School before going up to Christ Church Oxford in 1852, gaining his B.A. in 1856 and his M.A. in 1859. He trained for the ministry at Wells Theological College, being made a deacon in 1858, and he was priested by the Archbishop of York in the following year. He held curacies in Ledsham (Yorkshire) 1858-50, Budock (Cornwall) 1860-61 and Swindon (Staffordshire) 1862-67. He became priest-in-charge of Swindon briefly in 1867 before becoming

Vicar of Collingham (Yorkshire) from 1867-74. He first married (3 June 1862) Caroline Wheler, one of the daughters of his first vicar at Ledsham, by whom he had Hugh, his heir, another son and two daughters. At the time of his second (childless) marriage to Ingeborg Muller in 1902, he was still a clerk in holy orders, but he had not had charge of a living since he left his ministry in Collingham in 1874. After moving to Clowance in the late 1870s, he nevertheless assisted in the services and officiated as parish clerk and sidesman at Crowan church. He served as a magistrate and was a conscientious and energetic member of the Helston Board of Guardians for many years. He was a founder member of the Cornwall County Council, having been first elected in 1889 to represent the Sithney-Crowan Division, which he served for fifteen years. He described himself as a 'very liberal' Conservative who intended to serve the Council on 'lines of general usefulness, irrespective of party or creed'. He took a great interest in the activities of the Royal Cornwall Polytechnic Society; he was a member for more than fifty years and held office as Vice-President. He had a reputation as a generous donor to charitable causes, but he took only occasional part in the social life in the Falmouth area.

By Kind Permission of Michael Muller

Ingeborg Alfhild Muller, the first Lady Molesworth-St. Aubyn, was exceptional in several respects. She was not only the first to be so-styled, but she was also the first Molesworth/Molesworth-St. Aubyn consort not to be born in the United Kingdom; she was the first consort of a Molesworth/Molesworth-St. Aubyn baronet to have served as a Justice of the Peace in the county, and she is the only consort of a Pencarrow baronet (to date) to be honoured in her own right by her (adopted) country.

Ingeborg was the eldest daughter of the marriage of Johan Viggo Sigvald Muller (1836-1904) and his cousin Anna Schmidt (d.1896). Johan was a civil engineer who served his apprenticeship in England and, after his marriage, returned to this country to establish a family home in Fore Street, Newquay while he was engaged in building the Cornwall Mineral

Railway in the early 1870s, at which time he and his family became naturalized British subjects. He subsequently worked in, Turkey, Brazil, Argentina and Ecuador, before retiring to Newquay in 1899. Ingeborg was born in the Danish province of Jutland in 1870, and had three brothers, Osvald (1868-1916), who was Senior Wrangler of his year in 1890, and subsequently graduated from Jesus College, Cambridge, having taken a part II degree in History in 1891: In that same year, Arthur, two years younger than Ingeborg, was an undergraduate studying mathematics at Clare College, Cambridge, and her youngest brother, Hugh, was born in Newquay in 1877. She also had two younger sisters: Bothild (born 1874) and Thora (born 1875), both born in Newquay. By 1901, Ingeborg's mother had died, and only her father and her sister, Bothild, were still recorded as living in Fore Street. Of the subsequent history of the family we know only that Osvald became a professor at Elphinstone College, Bombay, but found time, and had the expertise while on leave from India to be involved in archaeological excavations at the pre-historic cemetery at Harlyn Bay, north of Newquay. Bothild subsequently married Professor Henry Dewey and they settled in Newton Abbott; Devon. Thora worked as a nurse, but never married and lived at Kilver Cottage, Newquay, and Hugh, a graduate of Emmanuel College, Cambridge, was ordained in 1901, served as a naval Chaplain during the war of 1914-18, and was Vicar of Appledore at the time of Ingeborg's death in 1928. He was quite a character and became something of a legend in his own lifetime.

On 2 September 1902, Ingeborg, with her address still given as Beaucliffe, Fore Street, Newquay, married the Revd. St. Aubyn Hender Molesworth-St. Aubyn of Clowance. At the time of the marriage, the bridegroom was a widower aged nearly 70, whose first wife had died three years earlier. The bride was aged 32, and was five years younger than her stepson Hugh, the future 13th Pencarrow baronet. After the marriage Hender and his wife lived at Clowance and, after he succeeded to the baronetcy in 1912 he, like his predecessor, Sir Lewis the 11th Bt., he chose not to occupy the mansion of Pencarrow which, after the death of Mary Ford in 1910, was reunited with the baronetcy from which it had been divorced for more than fifty years by the terms of the will (1855) of Sir William Molesworth, 8th Bt., Mary Ford's brother. The Molesworth-St. Aubyn's Clowance estate was sold and although the 13th baronet and his family moved to Pencarrow in Ingeborg's lifetime, it was not a decision nor a move with which she was in any way involved.

Ingeborg was widowed in May 1913 during a visit she and her

husband were making to London. After assisting at the morning service at St. Andrew's Church, Wells St., W1, Hender and his wife visited Chelsea Rectory to take tea with Archdeacon Bevan, Hender's cousin by marriage, when Hender had a seizure and died before medical aid arrived. He is buried at Crowan.

There are virtually no surviving records to tell us about Ingeborg's activities after she became an adult but, according to one tribute paid to her after her death, she used these years to travel widely in Europe, Asia and America, and she acquired the reputation of being an excellent linguist familiar with, if not expert in most European languages. After her marriage, as befitting someone in her station in life at the start of the twentieth century, she devoted herself to public service (increasingly so after her husband's death when she returned to live in Newquay) to the extent that a local clergyman wrote that there was no committee formed in the town to carry on beneficent charities or praiseworthy enterprises which was deemed to be complete, or likely to be successful, unless she was a member. She was a county magistrate, a Governor of the secondary school for girls, President of the Cornish Nursing Association, the Mothers' Union and the Girl Guides but, above all, she made her greatest impact in her efforts to establish Women's Institutes in the towns and villages throughout Cornwall and, during the war years 1914-18, her unstinting efforts to organize food production more efficiently and to recruit and train women workers in agriculture.

Ingeborg's obituarist in the Times of 13 December 1928 recognised her energetic efforts to make the lives of many women in rural areas in the county 'brighter and more useful.' In 1919, she was elected Founder-President not only of Newquay W.I., but also of the Cornwall Federation of W.I.s, and served in that capacity until her death. But her reputation also rests deservedly on the results of her efforts as Chairman of the Cornwall Committee of War Service for Women in co-operation with the Women's National Land Services Corps. She overcame the prejudice of the day which believed that women were 'too frail in body' to undertake the tasks on the farm which had traditionally been done by men. Many of the farm workers had gone off to the war and it was Ingeborg's task to convince farmers that women could most of the jobs on the farm quite as well as men, but she, and her female associates, were also insistent – well ahead of their time – that women so employed should earn a fair wage for the job. There is a record of Ingeborg travelling by train from Newquay in March 1916 to witness at Scarne Farm, Launceston, a demonstration of what women could do on a farm. The demonstration had the desired effect of proving that countrywomen were quite capable of all the tasks necessary for the growth and preservation of food. At the end of the day the women's work was judged to be quite satisfactory, and Ingeborg presented the prize money.

For her record of public service, her role in establishing Women's Institutes in Cornwall, and for her war work in the agricultural industry in particular, Ingeborg Lady Molesworth-St. Aubyn was appointed OBE in 1920. There are five photographic portraits of her taken in the Bassano studio in London after receiving her honour. The portraits can be located in the National Portrait Gallery, but they are not on display.

Ingeborg's influence was countywide, but it was principally felt in Newquay, the town in which the Muller family had settled when they arrived from Denmark, and to which Ingeborg returned after the death of her husband. She lived for the last fifteen years of her life in Atlantic House, Cliff Road, and her death was much lamented. In the words of a local clergyman 'she put all that she had at the disposal of Newquay and invested her time and talent for the good of the town and the welfare of its inhabitants.' There was, not surprisingly, a 'large and representative attendance' at her funeral service at St. Michael's Church in Newquay, but her final resting place was with her husband in the Molesworth-St. Aubyn family vault at Crowan.

The article about Sir St. Aubyn Hender and Lady Ingeborg Molesworth-St.Aubyn which appeared in a *Friends' Newsletter* 2007 came to the attention of Michael Muller, the great-nephew of Ingeborg, and he has supplied further pertinent details of the family, for which I am very grateful.

1. In the 1890s, Ingeborg took responsibility for the running of the family home, Beaucliffe House, Newquay, during her mother's illness, and after her death in 1896, for her father in his retirement

2. There is a record of Sir Hender and his wife going on a trip round the world c.1911, during which they stayed with Osvald and his second wife in India.

3. There are two windows (11a & 11b in the church guidebook) which commemorate Ingeborg's father, Johann, and his family in St. Michael's Church, Newquay.

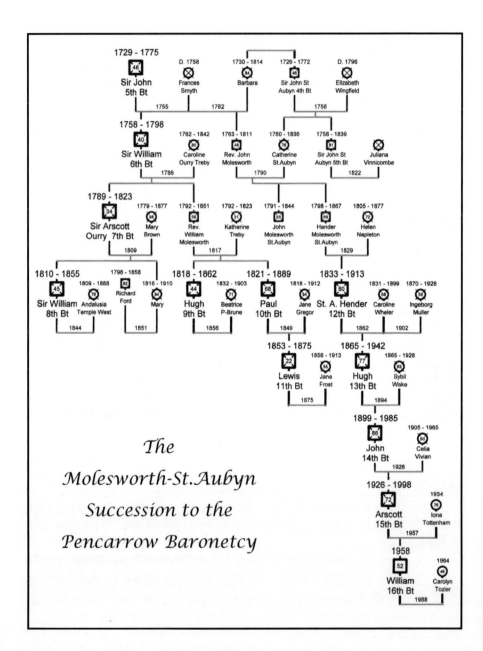

The

Molesworth-St.Aubyn

Succession to the

Pencarrow Baronetcy

The Wedding of the Future 13th Bart.[1]

On Tuesday 26th June 1894, Hugh Molesworth-St. Aubyn was married to Emma Sybil Wake in the church of St. Peter, Eaton Square, London. Hugh was the eldest son of the Reverend St. Aubyn Hender Molesworth-St. Aubyn and his first wife Caroline (née Wheler); Sybil (as she was known to differentiate her from her mother and her younger sister Emma Blanche) was the eldest daughter of the ten children of Admiral Charles Wake and his wife Emma (née St. Aubyn). The bride and groom were both twenty-nine years of age.

Sybil in her wedding dress

The marriage was celebrated at 1.30pm. and was conducted by the father of the groom assisted by the Reverend Edmund St. Aubyn, an uncle of the bride, and the church was decorated in tall palms and white lilies. Her father having died four years earlier, the bride was given away by Sir Hereward Wake, Bt., (her uncle). She wore a dress of rich white satin, trimmed with old lace, a full train and a magnificent Brussels lace veil. The best man was Mr Wentworth Ewing Cattley (a barrister colleague of the bridegroom), there were eight bridesmaids: the Misses Isobel, Emma and Christabel Wake (younger sisters of the bride), Miss Molesworth-St. Aubyn (sister of the groom), the Hon. Mabel St. Aubyn, Miss Wake (cousins of the bride), Miss Evelyn Schreiber and Miss Newton. Their dresses were of white muslin and moiré ribbons with large picture hats covered with red, pink and yellow roses, and they wore pearl swallow brooches, the gift of the bridegroom.

Amongst those present were: the Earl & Countess of St. Germans, Lord & Lady Robartes, Viscount & Viscountess Molesworth, Sir Hereward & Lady Wake, Mrs Molesworth-St. Aubyn, Mr Beville Molesworth-St. Aubyn, Mrs Ford (Pencarrow), Lord & Lady St. Levan, Mr & Mrs Edward St. Aubyn, Miss Juliana St. Aubyn, Major the Hon. & Lady Edith St. Aubyn, the Hon Otway & Mrs Cuffe, Mr & the Hon. Sidney Ponsonby, Mr & Mrs Schreiber,

Mr & Mrs Wheler, Miss Wheler, the Hon. Mrs Athelstane Riley, the Hon. Owen Molesworth, Count & Miss de Morel, Admiral Sir Houston & Lady Stewart, Mrs Basset, Mr & Mrs Pendarves, the Revd. & Mrs Rowland de Cerjat, Mr & Mrs Prideaux Brune &..

Owing to the death of a near relative, only those connected with the family were entertained afterwards by Mrs Charles Wake at 43 Brompton Square. Subsequently Mr and Mrs Hugh Molesworth-St. Aubyn – the bride wearing a going away dress of reseda crepon trimmed with blue chiffon and a hat to match – left by the 4.15pm. train from Paddington, en route for Malvern and Wales.

Surprisingly informative, the newspaper account ended with a list of the wedding presents and their donors: even more unusually, the presents were listed separately as presents to the bride and presents to the groom. As far as totals were concerned, the bride appears to have done better with 144 presents to the groom's 86 – moreover, Sybil was given a diamond ring by Hugh, whereas he does not appear to have received any gift from her! However, it must be emphasised that the accuracy of the account is clearly not foolproof, and the list cannot be considered to be exhaustive!

Most of the donors gave either to the bride or the groom, but fifteen gave individually to both, the presents of seven of whom were clearly intended as a joint gift - (e.g. napkin rings, an inkstand, a piano and a Chippendale chair). The bride's presents came under four headings:

> **Jewellery**: rings, pendants, bracelets, brooches & bangles (including a diamond & ruby brooch & earrings from the then chatelaine of Pencarrow, Mrs Mary Ford, which the bride, in time, would wear at Pencarrow when she became the chatelaine some 25 years later).
>
> **Personal items**: scent bottles, handkerchiefs, shawls, brushes, button-hooks, fans, handbag, purse, pincushion, thimble, dressing-bag, walking stick & a parasol.
>
> **Tableware**: two breakfast services, salt cellars, sugar basins, cream jugs, tea caddies, coffee pot, plates, dishes, junket bowl, basin, toast-rack, claret jug & 9 bonbonnieres!
>
> **Furniture**: writing table, oak table, two clocks (one miniature grandfather), eight vases, revolving bookcase, card table, two lamps, milking-stool, a picture by Bartolozzi [2], a set of reference books, two china dogs, a thermometer & – to recognise Sybil's interest in photography – a photograph (from her mother), seven photo frames, a wrought-iron photo easel & a photograph screen.

Sybil also received a volume of poems by Mathew Arnold and two cheques.

Hugh in militia uniform – a photograph not to Sybil's liking

Unsurprisingly, the bridegroom's presents were, in the main, traditionally male-orientated, and were made up of cigar boxes, cases, a cutter, matchbox case and holder, a decanter, flasks, wine taster, beer jug and four claret jugs. He was also given cuff-links, tie-pin, hunting crop, walking stick, letter-case, pocket-book, hat and clothes brushes a gold watch-chain (from his father), and a 'handsome kit bag' from his mother-in-law. But he, too, was given tableware – cutlery, tureens, salvers, dishes, jugs, salt cellars, condiment sets, a cake-stand, apostle spoons, a breakfast heater, a silver 'potato ring' and a dinner service from his best man. His bride was not alone in receiving items with which to furnish their home, since he was also given tables, chairs, a bookcase, two clocks, a barometer/thermometer, four inkstands, a statue, a cushion, a reading lamp, a set of engravings and, intriguingly, a tea-cloth! Finally, he will have been pleased to be given three cheques, since the first few days of the honeymoon were spent in what Sybil described as a 'frightfully expensive hotel' in Great Malvern.

In a letter to her mother written on the first morning of her honeymoon in reply to one Mrs Wake had written to her after the wedding the previous day, and which she had received in Malvern that morning (would that the postal services of today could match such efficiency!), Sybil wrote that the wedding day 'could not have been a greater success'.[3] She confessed that she was getting 'quite a start' whenever she was addressed by her married name, but she assured her mother that she and Hugh were 'utterly and entirely happy and there is no drawback. There is nothing more to be said.'

It may be that these comments were written purely as a reassuring statement of fact. However, from snippets garnered from the few of Sybil's letters (mostly undated and incomplete) which have survived from the relationship which she had with Hugh in the years immediately prior to their marriage, they could be interpreted as a dutiful, but nevertheless defiant, daughterly justification of her newly married status. Hugh and Sybil were distant cousins, and their families were close and on familiar terms – Sybil's first recorded letter to Hugh was addressed to 'My dear Hugh' and signed 'Ever your affectionate cousin, Sybil Wake – but Sybil's parents did not make it easy for her affection for Hugh (abundantly in evidence for at least six years before their marriage) to blossom. In May, 1889 Sybil wrote that her father had been critical of Hugh who, he thought, had unduly influenced her in some respect, but she was unable to give Hugh chapter and verse of the influence he was supposed to have exerted. Moreover, it is puzzling to speculate about the nature of the influence since Sybil wrote that it had been six months since she had seen Hugh, and that this was a letter written in reply to a letter from Hugh which, 'for once Mama has said I might answer,' but she suspects that permission to write again will not be readily given. Sybil bemoaned the fact that they were not allowed to correspond directly with one another – implying (in this letter and elsewhere) that letters may have been exchanged through third parties. She thanked Hugh for the photograph of him in Militia uniform which his mother had allowed to be sent with his letter to Sybil, and although she thought the photo was 'not good,' it was 'something to remind me of what you are like.' She lamented that time was passing slowly, that she longed to see him and she wondered 'when do you think things will come right {for us}', and she prophetically answered her own question with 'Not for ever so long, I suppose'.

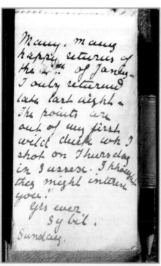

The first page of Sybil's 1891 diary/notebook

Two years later, Sybil kept a notebook/diary of her encounters with Hugh. In April, Sybil was invited to Clowance, where Hugh's mother was quite charming to her, and she described herself as the happiest person in the world. Hugh, the following month, visited Trevethoe (Lelant) for three days for his 'first real visit' to the Wake family who were staying there. The first day was described as 'lovely,' the second as lovelier and the third, needless to say the loveliest. There is mention of a joint family picnic at Gwithian but, in the main, Hugh and Sybil met at the houses of friends both in Cornwall (Glynn near Bodmin is mentioned more than once, as are Militia events and entertainments where Hugh looked 'awfully nice' in his uniform), or in the London town houses of friends from Cornwall (e.g. the Prideaux-Brunes in Charles Street). There is even mention of a visit to Oxford where one of Sybil's friends approved highly of Hugh, complimenting him on his nice manners, much to Sybil's satisfaction!

By this time, the terms of endearment in her diary are uninhibited, and Sybil refers to Hugh as her 'darling'; her letters are addressed to 'My own dearest Hugh', and she sends him 'all her love' but, as the following (undated) note from Sybil confirms, while reasonably free rein could be given to expressions of affection in writing, the lovers' social encounters were constrained:

'Good night, darling. Mama was so on the look out that I slipped up the backstairs and into my room to avoid any cutting remarks. You understood, didn't you? Mind and have a *good* night. I have had such a happy day. I never expected to be left so much in peace. Your own Syb.'

Hugh & Sybil shortly after their wedding

The restraints imposed upon the young couple were a reflection of the Victorian social mores rather than an indication of parental disapproval, although Hugh's lack of career and livelihood would have caused Admiral and Mrs Wake concern for their daughter's future well being. For all that Hugh would, in the course of time, inherit the Clowance estate, and was heir presumptive to the Pencarrow baronetcy and to the Pencarrow and Tetcott estates, Hugh's earnings as a young barrister in the 1890s would not have been assured. It was only when (c.1893) Hugh's father assigned to him Clowance Barton as a home, together with the prospect of making a living from the home farm, that his expectations became sound enough for Sybil's mother to give her formal approval for the marriage to take place.

Sybil well knew of the special relationship which existed between Mrs Molesworth-St. Aubyn and her elder son, and she was convinced that the Clowance Barton opportunity (and, consequently her marriage) had come about as a result of the influence she exerted over her husband, the Revd. St.Aubyn Hender. She felt indebted and became very close to her mother-in-law. So much so, that when the latter died in 1899, Sybil wrote to Hugh: 'Dear, dear mother, I can't believe I shall never see her dear face again. What shall we do without her?'

The marriage of Hugh and Sybil lasted thirty-three years until Sybil died after a long illness in 1929. Correspondence shows that the love they had for each other at the outset endured throughout the marriage, and that Sybil emulated her mother-in-law in one respect at least – in so much as her eldest son occupied a very special place in her affections. This is well illustrated in the weekly letters which she wrote and which chased John Molesworth-St.Aubyn on his travels in the nine months he spent undertaking a world tour in 1922. But that, as they say, is story for another day!

Sybil, her mother-in-law & eldest son,
John, at his christening, 1899

Notes & References

1   The first part of this article is based primarily on the account of the wedding printed in *The Western Morning News* on Saturday, 30 June, 1894, and the rest draws upon a notebook/diary written by Sybil & dated by her for 1891, and also letters written by her - frustratingly undated, but clearly all but one prior to her marriage.

2   In all probability an engraving by the Florentine engraver, Francesco Bartolozzi (1725-1815).

3   Mrs Wake had also written to Hugh by the same post.

The Consorts of the Molesworth Baronets
of Pencarrow, 1687-1912

As a result of three of the Molesworth baronets marrying twice, they contracted fourteen marriages in the two centuries separating Sir Hender, the first baronet, and Sir Lewis, the eleventh, and the last of that name before the baronetcy passed to the Molesworth-St. Aubyn branch of the family. Four of the consorts died before their husbands succeeeded to the baronetcy, consequently they were not entitled to be styled Lady Molesworth, and four who were so-styled never resided at Pencarrow, consequently they never enjoyed the status of chatelaine or mistress of the mansion.

Those who were never entitled to be called Lady Molesworth were:

Grace Tottle (née Mangey)

Daughter of a London goldsmith, widow of Captain Thomas Tottle, a merchant in Jamaica and **first wife of Hender 1st Bt**. She died 31 August 1687 and is buried at St. Ann's church, Soho, London. There were no children of the marriage. Her husband, Hender, was not created a baronet until July 1689, two years after her death.

Margery Wise

Daughter of Sir Thomas Wise of Sydenham House, Maristow, Devon, **first wife of John, 2nd Bt**., she was married 7 October 1663; died 19 June 1671, and was buried at Egloshayle. There were four children of the marriage: John, later 3rd baronet (23 June, 1668); a further two sons - Hender and Sparke, and a daughter, Mary. Margery's husband did not succeed to the baronetcy until September 1689, eighteen years after her death.

Margaret Slanning

Second wife of John, 2nd Bt., she was the daughter of Sir Nicholas Slanning of Maristow, Devon. She was born c.1642, married c.1675, died and was buried at Egloshayle 12 February 1682. There were no children from her marriage. Her husband did succeed to the baronetcy until 1689, seven years after her death.

Frances Smyth

Daughter and co-heir of James Smyth of St. Audries, Somerset, she was **the first wife of John 5th Bt**. She was married 28 September 1755, and died in childbirth 1 July 1758, having produced William, the future 6th Bt. Her husband did not succeed to the baronetcy until 1766, eight years after her death. She was buried at Egloshayle.

Those who were never Chatelaines of Pencarrow were:

Mary Lynch (néeTemple)

Daughter and co-heir of Thomas Temple of Frankton, Warwickshire, widow of Sir Thomas Lynch of Coker, Lt-Govemor of Jamaica, and **second wife of Hender, 1st Bt**. She was married 12 February, 1689 at St Martin in the Fields, London. Her husband died in August 1689; she died 11 July 1721: there were no children of the marriage. There is no record of her ever having visited, let alone resided at Pencarrow.

Beatrice Anne Prideaux-Brune

Youngest daughter of Charles and Mary (née Glynn) Prideaux-Brune of Place, Padstow and **wife of Hugh Henry 9th Bt**. She was born in 1832 and married 15 July 1856 in St. George's Hanover Square, London. She gave birth to one son, Hugh Prideaux 17 June 1857, but he lived for only a few hours; she subsequently gave birth to two still-born children (28 February, 1859, 28 March 1860). Her husband died 6th January, 1862 without leaving a son and heir to the title. She was the first Lady Molesworth to be denied the opportunity to live at Pencarrow as a consequence of the terms of the will of Sir William, 8th baronet, which alienated the baronetcy from the Pencarrow mansion and Molesworth family estates for fifty-five years (1855-1910), specifically the lifetime of his widow, Andalusia (d.1888), and his sister Mary (d.1910), the widow of Richard Ford, the celebrated critic and author, to whom he left a life interest in the property. After their marriage, Beatrice and Hugh lived at the Parsonage House in Little Petherick where Hugh was Rector of the church of St Petroc Minor. After Hugh's death, Beatrice lived mainly in London where she died 3 March 1903.

Jane Frances Gregor

Eldest daughter of Gordon W. F.B. Gregor of Trewarthenick, Cornwall, and **wife of Paul William**, who succeeded as **10th Bt**. on the death of his elder brother 6 January, 1862. She was born in 1818, married 25 July 1849 and was the second Lady Molesworth to suffer from the alienation of the baronetcy from Pencarrow. After their marriage Jane and Paul lived at Tetcott (north Devon) where Paul was Rector of the Molesworth family living of the Church of the Holy Cross. Their first child, Loveday Barbara, was baptised there (18 April, 1852), but Paul resigned the living when he was converted to Roman Catholicism in 1854. The varying birthplaces of the children of the marriage give some indication of the family's mobility in subsequent years: Lewis William (later 11th Bt.), Paul Francis and Katherine Maud Morwenna were born at the Gregor family home of Trewarthenick in 1853, 1855 and 1860 respectively. Mary Letitia was born in Clapham (London) in 1858, and Paul Francis aged only eight years was buried (1863) at Mortlake (London); In the early 1860s the family was at Kenegie, Gulval, near Penzance before taking over the lease of the Gregor family's seaside residence at the Tower, Newquay (the site of the present Newquay Golf Club), where Jane continued to live after Paul's death (23 December 1889) until she, herself, died 17th February 1912, aged 94 years.

Jane Graham Frost

Second daughter of Brigadier-General Daniel Marsh Frost, US Army, of St. Louis, Missouri, she was the **wife of Lewis William** who succeeded his father as **11th Bt**. in December 1889. She was born 23 December, 1858, and was only sixteen years old when she married in the Roman Catholic Church of St. Lawrence, St. Louis, 3 June, 1875. After their marriage they divided their time in England between Trewarthenick (Paul's mother's Gregor family property which passed by inheritance outright to Lewis in 1896), and a house in Great Cumberland Place, where they entertained a good deal in the London season. There were no children of the marriage. Lewis was a Fellow of the Royal

Geographical Society, and Jane shared his love of travel - they missed Mary Ford's funeral in 1910 because they were in Morocco. Lewis, having left Jane behind in Florence on their journey back from a tour in Egypt and Italy had himself returned only as far as Jane's sister's house, Vane Towers, Torquay, when he died suddenly and unexpectedly, 29 May, 1912. After her husband's death, Jane sold their town house and retired to Trewarthenick where, a year later 21 September 1913, she succumbed to a fatal reaction to a wasp sting. Both Lewis and Jane are buried Cornelly, Trewarthenick's parish church.

The Chatelaines of Pencarrow

Jane Arscott

Daughter of John and Prudence (née Dennis) Arscott of Tetcott, north Devon, born 19 June 1678, was the **wife of John** whom she married 19 July 1699 and who succeeded his father as 3rd **Bt**. in October 1716. She gave birth to seven children: Mary (April, 1703); John, (later 4th baronet) and his twin sister, Margery, (28 February 1705); Prudence (March 1706, who died aged six in 1712); Mender (May, 1709); Sparke (April, 1711) and Prudence (April, 1717 - May 1741). Prudence married Hugh Gregor of Trewarthenick whose descendant Jane Gregor married Sir Paul Molesworth (1849). When Jane's nephew John Arscott died (21 January 1788), he left no male heir and the Arscott estate at Tetcott passed to Jane's Molesworth great-grandson, William 6th baronet, by virtue of being the eldest surviving male descendant of Jane's father, John Arscott (1648-1708). She died 6 May 1719 and was buried at Egloshayle, as were her husband and all her children with the exception of Sparke who died at Naples (6 June, 1739).

Barbara Morice

Second daughter and co-heir of Sir Nicholas Morice 2nd Bt. of Werrington, north Devon, she was the **wife of John** who succeeded his father as 4th **Bt**. in June 1723 and whom she married 9 May 1728 at Crowan (her father having died in 1726, and her elder sister, Catherine, having married Sir John St. Aubyn Bart. of the nearby Clowance estate). By the terms of her father's will, she inherited £4,000 in addition to her settled portion of £6,000, and received a further £2,000 on the birth of her first male child. She gave birth to two sons and a daughter: John, later 5th Bt., (April, 1729) and William (October, 1732); her daughter, Catherine lived for only four years (1730-1734). Her sons married sisters, Frances and Anne respectively, daughters and co-heirs of James Smyth of St. Audries, Somerset. She died of smallpox on 17 April 1735 and was buried at Egloshayle.

Barbara St. Aubyn

Youngest daughter of Sir John St. Aubyn 3rd Bt. of Clowance, and **second wife of John, 5th Bt.** She was born in 1728 and married 22 July 1762 at St. George's Hanover Square, London. She gave birth to five children, of whom two only reached adulthood: John (1763-1811) and Hender (1766-99). Barbara (1765-71), Catherine (1768-69) and Sparke (1769-70) all died in childhood and were buried, as was Hender, at Egloshayle. Her eldest son became a clerk in Holy Orders and enjoyed in plurality the Molesworth family livings of St. Breock and St. Ervan. It was from him, as a consequence of his marriage to his cousin, Catherine, heir to her brother Sir John St. Aubyn 5th Bt., that the Clowance estate passed into the Molesworth family when Sir John died in 1839 without fathering a legitimate heir. John Molesworth's eldest son (also John, 1791-1844) inherited Clowance as the senior male of legitimate St. Aubyn descent on the death of his uncle, and assumed the additional name of St. Aubyn by royal licence after inheriting Clowance. Thus it was Barbara's great-grandson, the Revd. St. Aubyn Hender Molesworth-St. Aubyn who became the 12th baronet, the first of his branch of the family to inherit Pencarrow when Sir Lewis Molesworth died without leaving a male heir in 1912. Barbara died at Salisbury Mount, Heavitree, Exeter, 14 August 1814.

Caroline Ourry Treby

Born Caroline Ourry 26 June, 1761, she was the daughter of Charity (née Treby) and Paul Henry Ourry, M.P., but adopted the name Treby when the family changed surname on inheriting the Treby family property at Goodamoor, Plympton, Devon. She was the **Wife of William**, whom she married 27 May 1786, and who succeeded his father as **6th Bt.** in October 1775. She gave birth to three sons and two daughters, of whom Arscott

Ourry (1789-1823), later 7th Bt., William (1792-1851) and Caroline (1794-1872) survived childhood, but Frances (1787-90) and Arthur (1793) died in infancy. William became an Anglican priest, following his uncle by holding in plurality as rector the livings of St. Breock, St. Ervan and also Beaworthy, Devon. He married (1817) his cousin Katharine Treby (1790-1823), and was the father of Hugh Henry (1818-62) 9th Bt., and Paul William (1821-89) 10th Bt. In 1824, Caroline inherited The Lodge, Cobham, Surrey, from General Felix Buckley, one of the trustees of her husband's will, and she lived there after his death with her daughter Caroline. She died at Cobham 10 December 1842. In 1784, the year before her marriage, a barrister at the Assizes in Launceston was inspired to write the following lines on seeing her in the gallery:

At an Assizes at Launceston
Held before Judge Butter - 1784
Sir Wm Molesworth Bart. Foreman
Of the Grand Jury:

My Lord & Gemmen of the Jury
I come to prosecute before Ye
A noted felon I assure Ye
Known by the name of Carry Ourry
Known by a pair of guilty eyes
Guilty of fifty felonies
Guilty to push her crimes no further
Of stealing, killing, stabbing, murder

But to save time & cut it shorter
I but indict her for manslaughter.

When petty offences & Felonies smart ts
there no jurisdiction for stealing a heart?
You, Ourry, may smile & cry Laws, I defy
you
Convinced that no person can be
summoned to try you,
But think not such an excuse will secure
you
For the Muses & Graces will first make a
Jury

Mary Brown

The eldest daughter of Captain Patrick Brown, R.N., and his wife Mary (née Hume) of Edinburgh, born in 1779, and was the **wife of Arscott Ourry** whom she married in Edinburgh 7 July 1809, and who had succeeded his father as 7th **Bt.** in February 1798. There were six children of the short-lived marriage (1809-23), three boys and three girls, of whom two only lived beyond thirty years of age: William (1810-55), born in London and later 8th **Bt.**, the distinguished radical politician and philosopher, and Mary (1816-1910) born at Tetcott who later became (1851) the third wife of Richard Ford, the eminent critic and travel writer of the mid-nineteenth century. Mary was herself the chatelaine of Pencarrow 1888-1910, having been bequeathed a life interest in the property in the will of her brother, but she was not, of course, a Molesworth consort!

Of the remaining children, none reached the age of thirty: Caroline (1813-24) born in Edinburgh, died aged ten; Elizabeth (1811-36) born in London, Arscott (1813-42) born in Edinburgh and Francis (1818-46) born at Tetcott, all died in their twenties. During her long widowhood, Mary lived in Edinburgh in the 1820s and Pencarrow in the 1830s, but after her eldest son's marriage to Andalusia West (1844), she lived mainly in London, initially sharing a house with her daughter, Mary, at 6, Chester Street, Belgrave Square and then, after Mary's marriage, nearby at 14 Lowndes Street where she died 16 April 1877, aged ninety-seven, a widow for more than fifty years. Mary's mother was a renowned beauty. Mary and her two sisters clearly took after her - so much so that, in a newspaper cutting (sadly unattributed and undated) preserved in the Pencarrow archive is a 'Letter from an Admirer of the Miss Browns' in which he gives his opinion that the daughters of the 'beautiful' [former] Miss Hume are 'perhaps the most lovely women of the present day.'

Andalusia Grant West (née Carstairs)

Daughter of James Bruce Carstairs and Andalusia his wife, born in 1809, **married William 8th Bt.**, 9 July 1844, having previously been married (2 June 1831) to Temple West Esq., (1774-1839), of Mathon Lodge, Malvern, Worcestershire 'a gentleman well-known in fashionable circles' as he was described when the *Bath Chronicle* reported his death from a fit of apoplexy in April, 1839.

Prior to her marriage, Andalusia had been a student at the Royal Academy of Music in London (1824-27), and had won prizes for singing and proficiency in Italian. She first appeared by name in an Academy concert in 1826, and from 1827 until her first marriage, she performed on the public stages of Covent Garden, Drury Lane and the Assembly Rooms in Bath, adopting the name of Andalusia Grant. She regularly merited enthusiastic plaudits for her pure singing voice, but not for her acting on stage. Why she chose to be known professionally as Andalusia Grant is not known (Grant was, however, her mother's maiden name), nor is it known for certain how she and Temple West became acquainted but, as Alison Adburgham speculates in *A Radical Aristocrat*, her biography of the 8th baronet, Temple West was a lover of music and a generous subscriber of the concerts at the Academy and in Bath. This common interest may well have brought them together. Even more intriguing is the speed with which Sir William Molesworth became her second husband. There is no mention of Andalusia in William's diary or correspondence before he noted her address in his diary at the beginning of March 1844, shortly after he had returned to London having spent the previous three years at Pencarrow busy with his gardens and his edition of Hobbes's works and yet, barely three months later, they were married in St.George's Hanover Square. Because of her professional past, it was not a match which met with universal approval in the *beau monde* and, although they were initially welcoming and supportive, William's mother and his sister Mary came to despair of the effect that Andalusia's driving and unrelenting ambition to succeed as a society hostess was having on William, who had never enjoyed robust health, and whose political career was becoming increasingly demanding of his time and energy. When William succumbed to an untimely death at the age of forty-five, Mary, particularly, held Andalusia responsible, and had little subsequent contact with her until a reconciliation was effected in 1886 by John Venning, the Molesworth family solicitor, when it was thought that Andalusia was on her death-bed.

After the customary period of mourning the death of her husband, Andalusia's social life soon regained momentum. In London she vied with Frances, Countess Waldegrave as the leading society hostess and for a time in the late 1850s and 1860s, her house parties at Pencarrow in the late summer and early autumn were a successful extension of the London season and attracted visits from artists, musicians, authors, and poets as well as aristocrats and members of 'high society' - all, people and events, memorably recorded in the marvellous visitors' book on display today in the drawing-room at Pencarrow. But, as her visits to Paris increased, her visits to Pencarrow became less frequent - there were none between 1868-74, and only four 1876-88. There is little doubt that if Andalusia had been forced to make a choice of residence, Pencarrow would not have competed with her house in Eaton Place, London. It was here that she died 16 May 1888 and was buried in her husband's tomb at Kensal Green cemetery.

My Motoring Diary by H.M.-St.A.

Hugh Molesworth-St. Aubyn of Clowance, later to become the 13th baronet of Pencarrow, was 42 years of age in 1907 when he bought his first motor car, but his interest in automobiles had been aroused in the last years of the 19th century. In the 1890s he began subscribing to one of the earliest motoring magazines, *The Autocar*, and until his wife died in 1929, he collected the illustrations of exciting racing scenes and famous racing drivers of the day which were regularly published in the magazine. His fascination with every aspect of the transport he used – cost, mileage (for his 1¾ hp Humber motorcycle bought in 1903, and his Raleigh Model D and Golden Sunbeam bicycles on which he rode for nearly 2,500 miles between 1918 and 1928, quite as much as for his motor cars), performance, the specific attributes of each model together with its Treasury Rating – is dependably recorded in the diaries which he kept, copies of which survive from 1922 until his death in 1942. But, as well as incidental entries about transport in these journals, he also compiled a full record of all the cars he had owned, to the extent that we know the cost of each model, when and where it was bought, how it was disposed of, to whom and at what price, together with the specifications of each car. However, such was his infatuation for his first purchase that, from 1907-1911, he kept an additional specially designated journal, *My Motoring Diary,* to record his first four years as a car owner.

The car which Hugh bought through the Bickford Motor Company in Camborne from the Wolseley Motor Company in Birmingham, arrived by rail in Camborne and was delivered to his residence at Clowance Barton on Monday 6 April 1907. It was an 8hp., 9bhp., Wolseley, Registration Number AF 258. (Pictured at Clowance.)

Describing his purchase, Hugh noted that the car number was 1542; the chassis price at the Wolseley factory was £255; the car list price was

£315, reduced to £240. It eventually cost him, complete, £296. He went on to list knowledgeably and enthusiastically the car's special features – it had an M.6.V. exhaust (horizontal); 2 cylinders, 4 x 4, 900 revolutions per minute at which speed the 4 speed gear box gave speeds of 6, 12, 18 & 26 mph. It had an RAC rating of 12.8, with an ignition, electric accelerator and high tension coil; cooling pump and grilled tube radiator. Lubrication was by gravity and 8 sight feeds; petrol was fed by gravity. Transmission was by friction clutch in the engine with 2 drives to the gear box by Reynold's silent chain. There were roller chains from the sprockets on differential shafts to the car driving wheels. There were brakes on both back wheels, the wheels were of wood (artillery 30" diameter) and there were 3½" tyres. There were 4 forward and a reverse gear – speeds – reverse, neutral, 1,2,3,4.

Fortunately for the uninitiated and the novice mechanic (like the present writer!), he did not subsequently dwell upon technical details in his diary entries, but chose rather to record his journeys, his passengers, the routes followed, the weather, the road conditions, the mileage and other such mundane matters.

The first entry in the diary, 11 April 1907, reads 'First day I ever drove a Motor Car!'; the second, for 23 April, 'First day I took passengers!', and the third recorded that 1 May was the 'First day I ever drove alone!' In fact, from then on, he seldom drove alone. Much of the time his wife Sybil accompanied him in the car, and he also seemed to rely heavily and consistently on a driving companion he refers to in the diary by the initials A.B., whom it has been possible to name from another source as Arthur Burrall. However, quite who Arthur Burrall was, and what his relationship with Hugh was, is unclear. Burrall accompanied Hugh on his first car journey, so it must be presumed that he had some experience behind the wheel, and it is clear that he had some technical expertise for, when the Wolseley broke down at St.Erth after Hugh and Sybil set off for Penzance on 27 May, Hugh sent a 'friendly motor cyclist' to summon Burrall to mend 'a loose clutch pedal and overheated brake drums' which caused them a delay of more than 1½ hours on their journey. It would appear that Burrall was more of a socially acceptable and technically knowledgeable companion than an employee, since Hugh engaged James Goldsworthy to 'look after the car etc' on 1 June, and Goldsworthy replaced J.Hosken and C.Dally who had apparently been charged with the car's maintenance since its purchase.

Fortunately, the Wolseley appears to have been a reliable motor with very few mechanical problems. In addition to the St. Erth incident, Hugh wrote of difficulties in starting the motor on only a few occasions. The car spent three days in Bickford's garage in Camborne in June 1907 for some 'adjustments' to be made and, apart from mentioning that the car sometimes had to be 'rested' after climbing a steep hill, he recorded only three other incidents: on 16 October 1908 he had 'larger sprocket bolts fixed'; on 15 May 1910 he had a new speedometer fitted on 'Mia Cara'(as he put it!), and in August 1910 the Wolseley was taken to Bickford's garage once again to have new foot brakes fitted.

However, if the Wolseley's mechanical breakdowns were minimal, it has to be stated that the car was not over-used. Hugh laid it up for months at a time: 2 November 1907 - 7 September 1908; 25 December 1908 – 28 May 1909; 5 June 1909 – 13 August 1909; 10 August 1910 - 31 January 1911, and he does not record using the car after 29 August 1911 until the Wolseley was sold in June 1912, shortly after Hugh succeeded his father, Sir St. Aubyn Hender, as the 13th baronet. Moreover, even when not laid up, the car was not used for journeys of any great distance – a visit to a Garden Party at Tregothnan on 21 April 1910 involving driving 48 miles there and back to Clowance Barton is the longest journey recorded. The most regular use of the car was to ferry members of the family and house guests to and from Gwinnear Road Station to meet trains to Newquay and London, but the Wolseley was also used for visits to friends within the county but, destination apart, Hugh did not expand upon who or why he was visiting, nor what took place during the visit. There are occasional accidental mentions, for instance on a visit to Trengwainton on 30 August 1907, he witnessed a cricket match between Penzance and an All England XI (but we don't know the result) and on another visit there 22 July 1910 he attended a Garden Party in honour of the Atlantic, Mediterranean & Home Fleets of the Royal Navy which he described succinctly as a 'fine sight and a good day.'

Hugh was preoccupied with the performance of the Wolseley in a variety of conditions. Petrol consumption was not, however, a priority and was never mentioned. The state of the roads was often noted – 'very fair, but curly and narrow' on a drive to St. Anthony Head in September 1907; 'roads very heavy in places and very greasy' and although he described the route as 'much improved with the road widened' the hills and corners after Penzance were 'quite bad enough' on a trip to Land's End in October 1908 and, in 1909, he found the road 'very bumpy' between Helston and the Lizard. Ice was never mentioned as a hazard but, in March 1910, the roads were 'awful' after some snow had fallen, and he was constantly at pains to avoid loose stones in the road. Hugh was undoubtedly preoccupied with the length of his journeys, the time taken, the speed of his car and its ability to cope with the hills he had to climb - on several occasions he wrote of his delight at the way in which the car 'romped up the hills.' He wrote of the Wolseley averaging 15⅓ mph on a 3 hour journey to Land's End 'not bad considering the load (himself and two passengers), the [state of the] roads for an 8hp car!' On another occasion, on a journey to the Lizard, he calculated that he averaged $15^{21}/_{29}$ mph for the 38 miles, but it was with his average speed with which he was concerned, and not the maximum speed of which the Wolseley was capable.

In some respects driving for Hugh 100 years ago was far removed from present day conditions – for instance in October 1909, he drove all day and yet saw only 3 cars on his journey to and from the Lizard and Clowance Barton, and yet, in April of the following year, he encountered traffic chaos in Truro 'roads full of cattle and sheep', (one bullock charged the Wolseley and bent the off-side mudguard) and he thought that he had met 'every motor in Cornwall and every carriage in Truro.' In other respects, however, things have not changed much – Hugh was held up in Truro by road-works for the GPO and, on at least three occasions, he deliberately avoided driving along Hayle causeway 'owing to [prior warnings of] 'Police Traps'!

A month or so after the death of his father, Sir Hugh sold the Wolseley. He had owned it for just over five years, during which time it had suffered no major breakdowns or accidents. It was sold to S.J. Banbury of Camborne for £101, and the reading on the milometer registered a mere 1,327 miles – such bargains just do not present themselves in this day and age – not even on eBay!

Maudsley 17 (1911-13) AF709

Austin 20 (1923-9) AF7630

Arms.-Siddley 14 (1924-30) XU2621

A Ducal Service Rendered by a
Brace of Greyhounds

In 1066, the Duke of Normandy defeated King Harold in the battle of Hastings and was crowned William I of England. After his victory, he granted most of the lands of the defeated English nobility to his followers to be held by them for him on certain conditions, but primarily by Knight's Fee or Knight-Service, *i.e.* an undertaking to provide a quota of knights to serve in the field in the king's army for up to forty days a year, with specified armour, arms and a retinue, and none benefited more than William's half-brother, Robert, Count of Mortain. The count was granted nearly 800 manors spread across the country from Northumberland to Sussex, but his holdings (and his wealth) were principally centred in Cornwall where, when the Domesday book was compiled in 1086, he held the castles of Launceston and Trematon together with 248 manors, making him the first *de facto* if not *de jure* Earl of Cornwall.

Land barons like Count Robert safeguarded their ability to honour their Knight-Service obligations by assigning a portion of their fiefs or land-holdings to an under-tenant on conditions which varied according to the custom of each manor, but which were broadly similar to those by which they were granted their land by the king. This practice continued for another two centuries, until a change in the way wars were fought meant that mounted knights in armour were of less value to the king than foot soldiers, and the need for a more dependably funded army led to the development both of scutage, whereby a monetary payment was made in lieu of active military service, and to the custom of rendering payment in kind. By the time Edward III created his son, Edward, Prince of Wales, the first Duke of Cornwall in 1337, most of the 'services' of the manors in Cornwall had been commuted to money or in kind, and every seven years commissioners of the Dukes of Cornwall came to the gate of Launceston Castle to ensure that the conditions of the lease of the manors were kept, and that the customary dues and quit rents were paid. These visits lapsed with the passage of time and, despite the efforts made in the 1920s by Claude Peter, the Town Clerk of Launceston, and by Walter Peacock, the Keeper of the Records of the Duchy of Cornwall, it has not been possible to establish when the feudal dues were first presented to the Duke's commissioners not in money, but in the form of the following perquisites which were made in 1338:[1]

9 manors were required to present	1 pair of white gloves.
4 " " " "	1 clove of gillyflower (carnation)
4 " " " "	1 sore(?) sparrowhawk
2 " " " "	1 pair of gilded spurs
2 " " " "	1 pair of iron spurs
2 " " " "	1 rose
2 " " " "	wax – 1lb. and ½ lb. respectively

In addition, three more manors were each required to present 1lb. of cumin, a chaplet of flowers and 1lb. of pepper respectively, and one had to present two greyhounds and a hare. However, perhaps the most demanding perquisite was a total of 300 puffins expected from the Lord of Scilly.

The manor of Pencarrow, was listed in the Domesday Book of 1086, and was one of the Cornish Manors granted by William I, after his victory in the battle of Hastings in 1066, to Robert, Count of Mortain, one of seven landholders in the county. In 1086, the manor was held by Thurstan, the Sheriff of Cornwall, on behalf of the Count, but it is not clear whether it was held under an obligation of Knight-Service to the Count or the King. In any event, by the time the manor was purchased by John Molesworth in 1626, there is no trace of any such obligation, nor was it encumbered, like many Cornish Manors, with any commuted dues and none was ever exacted. However, the 1762 marriage settlement of Barbara St. Aubyn, the second wife of Sir John Molesworth of Pencarrow, the fifth baronet, brought with it the Lordships of the Manors of Elerky and Lanihorne in the Hundred of Powder and, with them, the commuted obligation to provide a greyhound from each Manor in lieu of Knight-Service to the Duke of Cornwall whenever he visited his Duchy.

There were no visits by a Duke of Cornwall to his duchy in the eighteenth century, but there were three visits in the nineteenth century. The future King Edward VII paid a fleeting visit to Restormel Castle on 23 July, 1865 and, in May 1880, he and his Duchess, the future Queen Alexandra, attended the part ecclesiastical, part masonic ceremonial of the laying of the foundation stone of Truro Cathedral. Seven years later, in November 1887, he returned with the Duchess to attend the ceremony to consecrate the quire and the transepts of the Cathedral. In 1865, he journeyed by carriage from his yacht moored in Fowey harbour to lunch at Restormel; he came to Cornwall by train to Grampound Road in 1880 when he stayed at Tregothnan, the seat of Viscount Falmouth, and, in 1887, he was again based on the Royal yacht, Osborne, in Falmouth harbour. Consequently, on none of these visits did he enter Cornwall by road via

86

Launceston, and there is no record of any dues being paid to him elsewhere in the Duchy on any of the visits.

The scene at the Gate of Launceston Castle prior to the arrival of the Duke

L to R: Sir Hugh Molesworth- St.Aubyn; Sir Trehawke Kekewich; Mr Edmund Lyne; Mr Bethner Hutchings; Mrs Christine Saunders.

Sir Hugh presenting the greyhounds

Although it is known that the future King George V and Queen Mary visited the Duchy as the Duke and Duchess of Cornwall in 1903,[2] according to official records it was not until the future King Edward VIII came to his Duchy in 1921 to attend the dedication of the War Memorial in Launceston, the ancient capital of Cornwall, that the question of reviving the ancient custom of paying the Duke his dues at the gate of Launceston Castle was raised by the then Town Clerk of Launceston, Claude Peter (Fig.1). It was he who established the list of perquisites presented to the Duke of Cornwall's Commissioners at the Inquisition at Launceston Castle in 1338 cited above, and in an exchange of correspondence with Walter Peacock, the Keeper of the Records in the London Office of the Duchy of Cornwall, the limited number of presentations[3] which were to be made to the Duke on the occasion of his visit on 25 May, 1921 was established. After an opening proclamation made by the Duchy Bailiff, there were eight presentations. First, by the Mayor on behalf of Launceston (100 shillings and 1lb of pepper); then the Mayor of Truro presented a bow of alder; and there followed presentations by the Lords of the following Manors or their representatives (Fig 2): Penvose (Sir Trehawke Kekewich, 1 pair of gilt spurs), Battens (Captain Stanhope Rodd, 1lb of cumin), Stoke Climsland (Mr. Edmund Lyne, a six-pronged salmon spear and a bundle of withy twigs), Swannacott and St. Mary Week (Mr. Bethner Hutchings, a goatskin mantle), Goscot (Mrs. Christine Saunders, a pink rose in bloom) and, for the Manors of Elerky and Lanihorne, Sir Hugh Molesworth-St. Aubyn presented the Duke with his 'rent' of two greyhounds, (named Dorothy and Minx. Fig. 3).

The representatives of the Manors at the gate of Launceston Castle

John Molesworth-St.Aubyn presenting the greyhounds

The next occasion on which the ceremony of the payment of dues took place was in 1937 during the visit of King George VI to the Duchy to commemorate the 600th anniversary of the creation of Edward, the Black Prince, as the 1st Duke of Cornwall. At that time, the Duchy was vested in the King who was the father of two daughters, but had no male heir, and he was only the third British monarch to visit Cornwall.[4] The ceremony which took place on 1 December followed the same ritual as in 1921, with the same perquisites and presentations (Fig. 4) from the Mayors of the Borough of Launceston and of the City of Truro, and from the Manors of Penvose (Mr. John Menhinick), Battens (Major Stanhope Rodd), Stoke-climsland (Mr. Stanley Langford), Swannacott and St. Mary Week (Mr. Bethuel Hutchings) and, representing his father Sir Hugh, John Molesworth - St. Aubyn Esq., presented two white greyhounds, named Spot and Nimbo, borrowed from Mr. Percy Hodge for the ceremony (Fig. 5). On this occasion, the Manor of Goscot was replaced by the Manor of Trevalga, represented by Gerald Curgenven Esq., who rendered 1 pair of white gloves and, *'The Manor of Cabilla held by the service of paying to the King one Grey Cloak as often as he should pass through Cornwall, and the Manor of Pengelly held by Sergeantry of receiving the Grey Riding Cloak when the King should be coming towards Cornwall and of carrying that Cloak with the Lord the King through all Cornwall'*- was represented by Viscount Clifden providing the Cloak, and having handed it to Mrs. Josephine Rolt, she made the presentation to the King. His Majesty then declared: *'I confirm you, and those you represent, Tenants, and give you and them peaceable and quiet seizin[5] and possession of the Manors, Lands and Tenements which you hold or represent according to ancient custom.'* The King presented a white rod to all who had rendered their symbolized Knight-Service, and the ceremony was concluded with the Bailiff declaring: *'Let every man depart and keep this day here upon a new warning and so God Save the King and the Lord of this Honour.'*

It is worthy of note that the Town Clerk of Launceston, (Stuart Peter, the son of the Town Clerk in 1921), did his best to obtain a symbolic pair of puffins to present to the King. Mr. Peter did not, for reasons unknown, seek them from the Isles of Scilly, but made an approach to Martin Coles Harman, the owner (and self-styled King) of the island of Lundy in the Bristol Channel. Mr. Harman expressed his willingness to help, but pointed out that while the Lundy puffins were plentiful (c.100,000) around Lundy between April and August, they were only to be found far out in the Atlantic for the rest of the year, and consequently were unobtainable in November and December. He wondered whether stuffed birds 'would do,' but Mr. Peter obviously did not consider that they would be suitable!

The next and most recent ceremony was held within the gate of Launceston Castle on 19 November, 1973, and marked the first official visit of Prince Charles to his Duchy. The procedure, the Manors represented (with one exception mentioned below) and their token rents remained as before, and were rendered on the day by the following: Viscount Clifden (the Manor of Cabilla and the Sergeantry of Pengelly); the Mayors of Launceston and Truro; Mr. M.W.B. Scurrah (Penvose); Mr. E. B. Latham (Battens); Mr. K.J. Uglow (Stokeclimsland); Mr. L.K. Hutchings (Swannacott and Week St.Mary); Mr. C.G. Peter (Trevalga), and Lt-Colonel J.A.Molesworth-St. Aubyn presented a brace of greyhounds on behalf of his father, Sir John. (Fig. 6)

The greyhounds were named Whisky and Soda, and were lent for the presentation by Mr. & Mrs. R.H.Parsons of Egloshayle, but on this occasion they were presented only for the Manor of Elerky *'held, prior to dismemberment.'* Quite when the 'dismemberment' from the Manor of Lanihorne took place has not been established, but there is a letter dated 10 November, 1937 in which Sir John Molesworth wrote to the Town Clerk of Launceston pleading a prior engagement which would make it impossible for him to pay his rent to the Duke in person, and there is a post script in which he says that after the 1921 presentations, Charles Henderson, the celebrated historian of Cornwall, had written that 'there was no foundation for my being Lord of the Manor!!' This challenging comment may well have led to a reassessment of the Molesworth-St. Aubyn's tenancies of the two Manors, but there is nothing on record to that effect.

The above would appear to be a full account of the twentieth century ceremonies for paying the token rents due to the Duke of Cornwall, but for the fact that, among the papers in the Pencarrow archive which record the proceedings of 1921, 1937 and 1973, there was found a tattered photograph which, when pieced together (Fig. 7), suggests that there may well have been a further, hitherto unrecorded ceremony. It appears to show a presentation being made by a person unknown to an unidentifiable couple in a setting which is so vague as to be unrecognisable! It looks as if the presentation is of a model white greyhound, together with a casket in which to house it, and the greyhound is mounted on a base on which there is a sadly illegible dedicatory/explanatory plaque. The costumes suggest that the period was Edwardian, and it is interesting to note that the future King George V and Queen Mary not only visited the Duchy in 1903, but paid a second visit as the Duke and Duchess of Cornwall in June, 1909. The likeness of the couple in the photograph to the royal couple is stretching credibility, but…

In 1903, The Duke and Duchess had been based at Tregothnan, primarily for ease of access to the ceremony at Truro Cathedral on 15 July, but they had also spent a day (17 July) 'motoring' through the Duchy – leaving Tregothnan at 11am by Tresillian, Ladock, Blue Anchor, Indian Queens, Goss Moors, Lanivet, Bodmin, Lanhydrock (where they had lunch), Restormel, Lostwithiel, St. Blazey, St. Blazey Gate, St.Austell returning to Tregothnan at 7pm. The following day (18th), the ducal couple visited Poldhu and the Lizard witnessing Marconi's wonderful wireless achievements, and being entertained to lunch by the Italian inventor. They also went by train to Plymouth to spend their last night (20th) in the Duchy at Mount Edgcumbe. However, at no point in their travels did they stop and receive any presentation.

In 1909, the Duke and Duchess were in Cornwall 8-10 June. They travelled by train from Waterloo to Bridestowe and then 'motored' (in a Daimler) to Polson Bridge where the royal party was welcomed by the Lord Lieutenant of Cornwall, the Earl of Mount Edgcumbe, who explained the ancient custom of presenting a grey cloak to the Duke. A newspaper account reported that 'there was a slight misunderstanding as to who should present the cloak. Lord Clifden as Lord of the Manor of Cabilla thought that, as such, he was entitled to present the cloak. Mrs. Lygon Cocks of Treverbyn, the Lady of the Manor of Pengelly, claimed priority of Lord Clifden, however, and the matter was referred to the Society of Antiquaries, who decided that Lord Clifden should provide the cloak, and that Mrs. Lygon should present it to the Prince.' The Duke and Duchess then motored on to Launceston where, at the Castle Gate, 'the Mayor (Mr. Kittow) presented an Address of Welcome. Ancient custom involved the *presentation of a pair of greyhounds and gold spurs, together with 300 puffins, ancient rent for the Scilly Isles. But these gifts were dispensed with. A white greyhound was to have been presented, but the owner was quite blind, and so this little ceremony was abandoned.'* [6] It is extraordinary that there is no reference to this 1909 ceremony in the 1921 correspondence concerned with reviving the ancient customs.

After tea in the Guildhall, the Royal couple left for Bodmin and then on to Newquay where they stayed at the Headland Hotel. On 9 June the Duke visited Padstow in the morning before, together with the Duchess, he travelled by landau to St. Columb Major to attend the Royal Cornwall Agricultural Show.[7] On the last day of their visit, the Duke and Duchess motored from Newquay via Roche, St. Austell, Lostwithiel, Liskeard, Cothele (for tea with the Earl of Mount Edgcumbe), before crossing the Tamar to Tavistock and arriving at Princeton to stay overnight at 7pm.

Loyal Addresses and presentations were made at Bodmin and Newquay on 8 June and, at the showground the following day, a newspaper account recorded that the Duke received an 'Illuminated Address of Welcome enclosed in an oak casket made from old oak taken from St. Columb parish church when it was renovated. On each of three sides were respectively carved the Duke's arms, the Prince of Wales's feathers and the Cornish arms. The remaining side bore representations of the industries of the county – fishing, agriculture and mining. The cask was heavily mounted in silver gilt.' This casket clearly does not match what is shown in Figure 5, but neither do descriptions of the other presentations made during this short visit, and so the puzzle remains unsolved.

Was there another presentation? If so, when and where, by whom and to whom - or does the photograph record the rehearsal of a presentation which never actually took place? It may be that the questions posed by the event illustrated in Figure 5 are too buried in history ever to be answered, or perhaps the mystery may be solved when files are re-opened in preparation for the ceremony when the next Duke of Cornwall receives his token perquisites on his first official visit to his Duchy. We can only hope that an explanation of what is pictured in Figure 7 will be forthcoming but, in the meantime, we have a constant reminder of the perquisites rendered at the Gate of Launceston Castle in an exhibition permanently on display in the Museum in Lawrence House in Launceston.[8] On view are the token rents – the bow of alder, the grey cloak, spurs, salmon spear and bundle of withies, the goatskin mantle, the pepper, cumin and the white gloves. There are no greyhounds, however, either stuffed or as carved or drawn models, but they have not been forgotten and are imaginatively remembered in a display of two handsome dog-collars.

Notes & References

1 I have been privileged to get a sight of the correspondence in 1921, between the Town Clerk of Launceston and the Keeper of Records of the Duchy of Cornwall (when the former was keen to re-establish the custom of paying dues on the occasion of the visit of the Duke in May of that year), and also subsequent correspondence in 1937 held in the archive of the Lawrence Museum in Launceston. I am very grateful for permission to draw on this correspondence for material for this article.

2 The Duke had already visited the Duchy when, as Prince George, he had accompanied his parents when they laid the foundation stone of Truro Cathedral in May 1880.

3 It was estimated that those represented amounted to 3% of the Duke's old established Cornish Manors.

4 Charles I had come in 1646 to stiffen the royalist cause in the West Country, and Queen Victoria with the Prince Consort two hundred years later had touched land in the Duchy from the royal yacht at Mount Edgcumbe and Fowey and, like her son in 1865, had paid a brief visit to the royal castle of Restormel.

5 Seizin – feudal possession of a freehold estate or land.

6 Author's italics and bold type.

7 I am grateful to Mrs. 'Billy' Glanville of St.Columb Major for the information she provided about the ducal visit to the Royal Cornwall Show.

8 Lawrence House, 9 Castle Street, Launceston is open to the public on weekdays from early April until late September. Entry is free.

John Clift and Pencarrow in the late
18th & early 19th centuries

In 1991, a collection of letters written by members of a Bodmin family was published.[1] The editor of the collection, Dr Frances Austin, was drawn to the letters by her professional interest in the English Language, and her research was rewarded by the discovery of a rare and rich mine of material indicating the extent to which language was in the process of change in the fifty years covered by the correspondence. There is also much in the letters to attract the social historian, since they paint a lively, vivid picture of life in the late eighteenth and early nineteenth centuries in both country and capital, as seen mainly through the eyes of what Dr Austin calls a 'substratum of ordinary people'. But for anyone interested in Pencarrow, the collection contains letters written by an estate carpenter which, together with comments and references in other letters written by his brothers and sisters, shed light on life at Pencarrow at the turn of the nineteenth century. These glimpses have been enhanced by the rewarding discovery in the Molesworth St. Aubyn papers in the Cornwall County Record Office of a bundle of contemporary estate accounts.[2] Unfortunately, the accounts are neither complete nor very detailed, but they are nevertheless informative and illuminating.

The Clift Family Correspondence is a collection of letters written by the six children of the marriage (29 February 1756) of Robert and Joanna (née Courts) Clift. Robert (1725-84) came from Altarnun, and Joanna (1733-87) from Cardinham. Robert was a miller, first at Glynn, near Cardinham, where the four eldest children were born - Elizabeth (1757-1818), John (1759-1819), Thomas (1762-1835/6) and Joanna (1765-1846) - and then at Burcombe Mill, nearer Bodmin, where Robert (1768/9-1799) and William (1775-1849) were born. None of the letters shed any light on the lives and characters of the parents, nor do they reveal any particulars of early family life, but William, writing years later in 1840, wrote of his father that he 'could read well, and write very tolerably', something few of his 'compeers' could do at that time. William added that his father had struggled to make a living as a miller and was ultimately forced to give up the mill and find work where he could as a journeyman miller. William's mother and sisters were out-workers, earning fourpence a day spinning and carding wool at home, and this helped to pay the weekly threepence needed to pay for William's elementary schooling until his mother's death in February 1787, shortly before his twelfth birthday.

It was clear from an early age that William possessed a talent for drawing, and this may have encouraged an investment in his education. At all events, it was William's artistic ability and penmanship which brought him to the attention of Mrs Nancy Gilbert, the daughter of a former Vicar of Bodmin and chatelaine of the Priory, the big house of the town. She became William's benefactress, and recommended him as a suitable apprentice to a former schoolmate who had married the eminent surgeon and anatomist, John Hunter, whom she knew was looking for an amanuensis to assist in drawing specimens and writing from dictation. In February 1792, William set out for London and the start of an apprenticeship which led to a career which would see him appointed the first Conservator of the Hunterian Museum (the incomparable collection of anatomical and biological specimens collected by his master, the founder of modern British surgery) in 1799 and, in 1823, achieve the distinction of being elected a Fellow of the Royal Society. It is to William Clift we are indebted for the preservation of the 138 letters that constitute the published collection, and which are located in the William Clift papers deposited in the British Library[3], the British Museum (Natural History)[4] and the Library of the Royal College of Surgeons of England.

None of William's brothers or sisters succeeded in breaking away from the social milieu into which they had been born. It is not known whether, like William, their parents were able to afford the fees for their basic education, but there is some evidence that they all received some basic instruction and encouragement to master their three 'Rs' at home. Writing to his son-in-law in 1845 and looking back to his youth, William recalled the following advice given to him by his eldest brother, John. 'Don't think or care so much about Fine Writing as attention to your Spelling. The finest Writing will be little valued if the spelling be defective.' From their letters it is evident that this was advice that both John and William bore in mind. It was clearly not a preoccupation with their brothers and sisters, but even their letters suggest that they were at least as literate as William claimed their father had been.

Elizabeth never married and, after the death of her mother in 1787, kept the family home going in Castle Street, Bodmin, until 1794, when she was evicted. She subsequently went into domestic service in Penzance, Launceston, and then together with her sister Joanna in Plymouth, before going to be nearer her younger brothers Thomas and William in London in

94

1802. Sixteen years later she returned to Cornwall to live with her sister, Joanna who, by that time, had married and left London with her husband for Gerrans, and Elizabeth died there later that year.

Joanna went into service at an early age and found positions in Bodmin, Liskeard, and Plymouth before going to London in 1800, where she was in regular contact not only with William who had urged her to move to the capital, but also rather more with another of her brothers, Thomas, and his first wife. She appears to have changed her employers fairly regularly, for the Correspondence shows that, in her early years in the capital, she had addresses in Hoxton, Shoreditch, Long Acre and Cornhill. By 1812, she was married to Thomas Honey, part owner of a Cornish fishing boat, and subsequently (c.1817) she returned to the West Country to live at Portscatho near Gerrans. Fifteen years later, she wrote to William from an address in Truro where she had moved, possibly because her husband's health was failing. In 1842, after his death, Joanna married Thomas Soady, a shoemaker from Bodmin whom she had known since childhood, and returned to live in a house in Turf Street in that town, where she died four years later aged eighty-one, estranged from her second husband.

Of two of William's brothers, Thomas and Robert, little is known, and they contribute few of the collected letters - both are quoted as saying that they have written more letters, but that these have gone missing. When the correspondence begins, Thomas was a cordwainer working in Bristol; he moved subsequently to Southampton before finally settling in London in July 1796. By the time his sister Joanna moved to London in July 1800, Thomas had married his first wife, Mary, (probably early in 1798) and had one child. After Mary's death, Thomas remarried (c.1818) and continued to live and work as a shoemaker in the capital until his death in 1835, at the age of seventy-three. Robert enlisted in the Royal Navy in May 1790, and had something of a chequered career, including active service in the Mediterranean, deserting his ship and then remustering under a different name before he drowned in the West Indies in July 1799.

Pencarrow is mentioned in letters from Elizabeth and Joanna. Both sisters are known to have visited John at Pencarrow, and William is known to have done so on at least one occasion, but it is, unsurprisingly, John, who is the principal source of information about Pencarrow. This is provided not only in his letters, but also in an incomplete sheaf of estate accounts for the years 1797-1809 in which he regularly features.

John Clift, the oldest brother, wrote eighteen letters in the collection of the family correspondence; only Elizabeth and William penned a greater number. His letters are all written to his youngest brother, and there are also copies of three letters from William to John, and a letter of condolence from William to John's widow after his brother's death in 1819. None of the letters shed any light on his early years. Nevertheless, John's handwriting, his level of literacy, the turn of phrase in his letters, and the intellectual curiosity he revealed in a letter written in 1798 when he disclosed that he was subscribing to weekly instalments of the Universal Dictionary of Arts, Sciences and Literature, suggest that he may have had as much early

Ford Augt 11 – 99

Dear Brother/

I suppose long before this time you must think I have entirely forgot you but believe me my love for you is just the same, though so long since you had a Specimen of my remembrance. I shall not set about finding excuses but own my fault, & hope you will forgive my neglect in time past, I have deferd writing so long I am almost asham'd to write at all but it I hope, never shall be the case again, I did not know of Mr Gilberts going to London till just as they returnd. I happend to be at Bodmin when William returnd at Mrs Tabbs I were Just got in to the house speaking to Mrs Tab when the Coach stop'd at the door, I went out to see who the Pasengers were as I thought it might be some person or persons I knew I met a young man at the Door who took me by the hand and askd me how I did (it being very dark I did not know him at first but on entring the house he was soon Surrounded there was Mr T Pearce desirous to hear from his son Thos, who I find is in London

I am still at Pencarrow as usual but
shou'd be much happier if the family were
here as usual, when I lost Sir Wm I lost a
good Master & a True friend but its vain to
repine — I hope I shall do verry well if please
God to bless me with health

Sister Betty called on me at Christmas as she
return'd from Penzance she slept at our house
at Mrs Jefferys — one night I wou'd have had
her stay longer but she wanted to be at Plymo
as soon as posable, I went as far as Bodmin
with her, I slept in Town one night & return'd
the next morning, I expected she wou'd have
staid 3 or 4 days at Mr Eyres they were
verry kind to her & desir'd her to stay for a
week I promis'd her to come again to Bodmin
before she went but before the time appointed
she was gone & I have not heard from her since
There is a Camp on Bodmin Race Ground in which
is the Artillery, the Stafford, Millitia the Radnor
Do & Cornish Supplementary Do it is the first of
the kind I ever saw I think its a verry
pretty sight Wm Tabb always enquires for you
& desires to be remember'd to you, I hope shall
hear from you soon so I must conclude with
my best wishes for your Health & Prosperity and
am with great respect your Afectionate Brother
Jn Clift

A Copy of a letter written by John Clift

schooling as his youngest brother and profited from it. Like his maternal grandfather, John became a carpenter and served his apprenticeship with Richard Tabb at Pencarrow - he mentioned his 'engagement' to him, in a letter of August 1793, and he referred elsewhere to Tabb as 'my old master'.

John's letters do not reveal any very close relationships with others in his family and, illness apart, he was quite sparing with news about himself. For example, at the age of forty-five, John married (9 April 1804) Anne

(Nancy) Menhennit (Menhinnet?), the dairymaid at Pencarrow, and he didn't even inform William of the marriage until a year later - in fact, none of his family was present at the ceremony which was witnessed by two fellow Molesworth tenants, John Deny of Ford and Stephen Hoare of Sladesbridge. John's early letters to William were newsy and solicitous enough, but seem to have been written to a template of 'elder brother' to 'younger brother' exhortations. The fact that William copied only three of his letters to his elder brother could be taken to indicate that he did not often write to him, or that the letters he wrote were not worth copying into his letter-book, but it is worthy of note that, once established in the capital, William invited his sisters to join him in London, but no such invitation was ever forthcoming for John.

John and Elizabeth were not close. Elizabeth thought John idle, irresponsible, lacking in concern for his family, unreliable and rather more fond of visiting public houses than of visiting her when he came to Bodmin and yet, when John fell seriously ill in November 1795, Elizabeth rushed to his bedside at Pencarrow and stayed until he had recovered. John, for his part, considered his elder sister to be rather sanctimonious, and too inclined to be censorious of the foibles of others, particularly his own. Nevertheless, it has to be said that Elizabeth's opinion of her brother was shared by at least one other, a family friend, Elizabeth Yeo. John had been her 'beau' when William had left for London in February 1792, and William expected them to be 'almost married' when he wrote his first letter to John from the capital some months later. Nothing came of the relationship, however, and Elizabeth Yeo wrote to Elizabeth Clift in February 1801 to say that she had not seen John for the previous three years, and had no wish to renew contact with him, as she was still of the opinion that he was 'very idle', uncaring and spendthrift. There is no surviving correspondence between John and the rest of his family but, in letters from Joanna to William in 1819 and 1820, Joanna wrote movingly about the deaths of her sister and brother, and she clearly had tender feelings for both of them. She had grown closer to John in the last years of his life and had stayed with John and Nancy in their cottage at Pencarrow only a few months before he died. William, too, after a very brief meeting with his brother at Pencarrow while he was staying at the Priory in Bodmin in 1813, was sufficiently concerned about John's health to send him stockings and gloves for the winter, and to consult an eminent surgeon about his brother's gout. He forwarded the surgeon's 'memorandum' about John's 'mode of living' and hoped that it would be of 'material service' to John. By contrast, William's letter of condolence to John's widow was rather cool and formal. He expressed regret at not having written to his brother more recently/frequently, but merely referred to the news of John's death as 'unwelcome' tidings, although he was happy that John, after years of suffering, was not in great pain 'towards the last'.

John Clift was born in the mill at Glyn and was baptised in Cardinham church on 30 September 1759. It is not known when he began to work at Pencarrow, but he was certainly lodging on the estate when the correspondence starts in February 1792. However, in a letter written in October of that year, he mentioned having just finished working for a Mr Chapple, engaged upon a task which had taken him one year and three-quarters to complete, and for which he had yet to submit his account. He wrote of his resolution to be more business-like and not to let matters drift for so long in the future, but to balance and submit his accounts monthly. A Mr Chapple figures in the estate accounts for 1808, when he was paid for having surveyed properties in the Molesworth estate, and it is known from other sources that there were two surveyors called William and James Chapple active in Bodmin at that time, but it is not clear to which John Clift was alluding. At all events, John made no further reference to Mr Chapple but, in the October 1792 letter, John wrote that Sir William Molesworth [6th baronet] had placed an order with him for more work than he had ever had before. Possibly as a consequence of this order - which was to make furniture for a house in London which Sir William was having built in 'Mary Bone Fields, Westminster' - he disclosed some ill-feeling between himself and Mr Tabb who may have felt slighted by the commission given to his erstwhile apprentice. Richard Tabb may well have been the carpenter 'in residence' at that time (an inventory of Pencarrow House carried out after the death of the 6th baronet recorded that he had had a room allocated to him in the house). John Clift's contribution as an employee was clearly valued for, after Tabb's death at the age of sixty-five in November 1796, he was appointed to take his place. In July 1799, Elizabeth Clift wrote that, when the House was closed up after the death of Sir William Molesworth, her brother was entrusted with looking after the building with instructions to do what he could to 'Ceep it in repare'. Some estate accounts have survived for the years following John Clift's Pencarrow advancement, - regrettably they are incomplete, but they exist in part or whole for the years 1797-98, 1802, 1806-08 and 1809 and, in these, despite his added responsibilities, the payments were always made to John Clift, carpenter, They are reproduced in the table on the following page.

Date	£	s	d	Date	£	s	d	Date	£	s	d
1797 2 Dec	29	19	6	**1802** 31 Dec	5	5	11	**1808** 17 Oct	8	15	6
1798 15 Feb	3	2	4	**1806** 11 Jul	0	13	6	" 31 Dec	7	17	6
" 28 Aug	14	2	4	" 10 Oct	1	16	0	**1809** 12 Apr	6	15	0
" 16 Nov	4	10	6	**1807** 3 Oct	7	9	7½	" 20 Jul	7	15	3
1802 4 May	8	4	2	" 31 Dec	6	1	6	" 9 Oct	7	19	9
" 1 Sept	7	5	3½	**1808** 10 Apr	6	8	3	" 30 Dec	7	19	9
" 2 Nov	4	0	0½	" 8 Jul	8	11	0				

The above totals were invariably accompanied by the words 'as per bill' which suggest that an element of the amount paid can be attributed to the cost of materials. Richard Rundall, a carpenter also retained by the Pencarrow estate, and to whom payments are recorded 1797-1802, was paid an annual wage of 18gns, but he was older than John Clift (he had been a witness to the marriage of Robert Allanson, the supposed architect of Pencarrow House, in 1766), and had almost certainly been employed for longer at Pencarrow. In John Clift's case, the payment of £3.2s.4d. in February 1798 was itemised merely as '3 months to 31 December 1797', suggesting a daily wage of 8d., £1.0s.9d. monthly, or a yearly wage of £12.9s.4d. Evidence from the estate accounts suggest that the Molesworths were not parsimonious employers. They were, for example, paying their maidservants annually between 8gns and l0gns for board and wages when the 6th baronet died in 1798, at a time when John Clift's younger sister, Joanna, employed in a similar capacity elsewhere in the county, could earn a wage of only 50 shillings in 1793-4, rising to 3gns from a subsequent employer in 1796-7.

John Clift also spent some of his time working as a house painter at Pencarrow and on some of the estate properties. He wrote in 1800 that it had been Sir William's pleasure 'to put me with Several Painters to improve in that business,' and he added that he had been working 'mostly in that way' for the previous two or three years. In a previous letter, he made it clear that it was not an occupation which he found either appealing or healthy. While painting a house belonging to Sir William at Tregonna [Little Petherick], near Padstow, he had been made ill by the poisonous fumes given off as he mixed the colour of bright green paint which Sir William's wife, Lady Caroline, particularly requested. 'I hope I shall never have another such Jobb' was his fervent wish in 1797, but it was not to be, for he wrote subsequently of painting Mr Tabb's house in Bodmin, a property at St Kew for the Pencarrow Steward and then, in 1800, he informed his brother that he had a long and troublesome job in the 'painting line' ahead of him in the summer of that year. It is also probable that, in the years that Pencarrow remained closed between the death of the 6th Baronet in 1798, and the first visit of the 7th Baronet, Sir Arscott, in 1812 after he had attained his majority, it was painting quite as much as carpentry which occupied him during that time.

At some time before 1817, in addition to the manual work for which he had been initially retained, John Clift had assumed greater and more general responsibilities at Pencarrow as a sort of clerk of works, super-intending all the work and keeping account of all that was brought in and carried out of the house. Eventually, after a particularly severe attack of gout, he was released from all manual work and, for the last two years of his life, was appointed by Sir Arscott Molesworth and his wife, Lady Mary, to act as the intermediary between them and the tradesmen with whom they had dealings at Pencarrow.

Although John Clift made some use of the family's cottage in Bodmin until his elder sister was forced to give it up in 1794, he was lodging at Pencarrow from at least the start of the correspondence in 1792. From 1795 until 1799, he had accommodation with the coachman, Richard Jeffery and his wife Nancy. In 1800, he wrote to William that he was lodging with the gardener, 'Mr Bevan' [George Bavin] in the gardener's cottage, where he was very content with his lot. 'I have washing, lodging, making/mending, milk for breakfast... and all kinds of Garden stuff of the best for 1/6d per week'. After his marriage in 1804, he and his wife moved to a cottage at Pencarrow where they were able to keep a pig and a cow, and he wrote that they were living 'verry happy' although, as Joanna later wrote to William, he came to find the stairs in the cottage tiresome in the last years of his life.

In common with all the letters written to William in London from the members of his family still based in the West Country, John's letters contain information (and gossip) about friends and relations, whom William would have known in his youth, news about proceedings at the Assizes in Bodmin, and also share a preoccupation with the health of the writer and of mutual acquaintances. In this last respect, John was at pains to dispel the rumour that he was too fond of the 'demon drink'. Although he admitted to drinking gin in 1793, five years later he boasted that he very seldom drank anything but 'tea or clean water'. By 1800, he believed that his experience could prove it was a fallacy that drinking alcohol to excess brought on 'the Gout', for he seldom drank 'any sort of liquor, especially spirit', and yet he continued to suffer from attacks of gout. The treatments which John wrote of taking to cure his various ailments - Rochelle salts, magnesia, chamomile flowers, pills made of 'Assafatida, Aloes, Rhubarb and Castile Soap' and the 'effect of electricity' (which produced a miraculous improvement in his health in 1806), would interest a medical historian.

The boundaries of John's world were limited. He had hoped to go to London in 1794 with the furniture which he had made when it was shipped to the capital from Fowey, but he was not allowed to go. This decision by Sir William Molesworth was perhaps influenced by Mr Tabb's opinion that 'there are too many publick houses for him [John] to do well there'. As far as is known, he travelled only as far afield as Fowey, when he saw William off on his voyage to London, and to Plymouth to visit Joanna when she was in service there, but he described happenings of moment locally which were both socially significant and remarkable: prices of basic foodstuffs, the corn riots in Padstow in 1793, the camps on Bodmin racecourse in 1798 for the artillery and the militia, and the presence of a great number of French prisoners in Bodmin in the 1790s. It is only to be regretted that his letters did not contain more information about the Molesworth family and Pencarrow at the turn of the nineteenth century.

As a mere artisan retained for work on the House and the Pencarrow estate properties, John Clift can have had little direct contact with Sir William Molesworth, 6th baronet. Richard Tabb was clearly his immediate supervisor at Pencarrow until his death late in 1796, and John will have taken his orders from him and not directly from the 6th baronet. He did not hold a grudge against Sir William for not sending him to London, for he wrote sincerely that he was a 'good and worthy master', and the sorrow which he expressed at the baronet's death in February 1798 was undoubtedly genuine. He wrote well of Sir Arscott, the 7th baronet who, together with his wife, Lady Mary, were 'constant visitors' at his Pencarrow cottage when he was incapacitated by a severe bout of gout in 1817. He was treated by the Molesworth family doctor, and they were compassionate about his poor state of health to the extent that, after he had recovered, they insisted that he should do no more manual work, but be employed in future in a purely supervisory capacity at Pencarrow. Sir Arscott further assured William Clift that John would 'never want for anything in his power'. Although Sir Arscott was in Scotland at the time of John's death in 1819, he was as good as his word as far as John's widow, Nancy, was concerned. Joanna wrote in 1820 that, although she was still the dairymaid at Pencarrow, and had a great deal of other work to do, to the extent that she was a 'complete slave' when the Molesworths were in residence, Nancy was well-liked by the family, and Sir Arscott, and subsequently his widow, Lady Mary, allowed her to continue to live on the estate for a further twelve years until her death in 1829.

It is not possible to establish accurately the extent to which the Molesworths were 'in residence' at Pencarrow during the years under consideration. It is obvious from the references in the *Correspondence* to Sir William's actions as a local Justice of the Peace, that he was 'in residence' for much of the year, but his parliamentary duties as MP for Cornwall, like his father, grandfather and great-grandfather before him, required him to spend time in London and to have a London address. It must also be kept in mind that he had inherited Tetcott in Devon in 1788 and he must, surely, have visited that estate also. In an early letter John Clift wrote that his master had a London house off Portman Square [now W1 but, when built c. 1770-80, this was a development on the outskirts of the city] and also that, in the early 1790s, Sir William was commissioning new furniture for a house he was planning to have built not far distant in Mary Bone fields. This was an area [now known as Marylebone] which was developed as a residential site in the last years of the century. It is likely that Sir William's family spent some months each year (possibly winter and early spring) in the capital, for we know that they returned from Portman Square in May 1792 after John had been busy putting Pencarrow in order in preparation for their arrival. We know, too, that the family left Pencarrow for London in February 1794 and that Sir William died in London in February 1798, but it is not clear when or if the move from Portman Square took place.

The death of Sir William led to changes at Pencarrow. Four of the servants were discharged including the coachman, the groom, a housemaid and the laundry maid and, as John Clift remarked 'there will not be much doing at Pencarrow for the next twelve years' - i.e. until Sir William's son, Arscott, the 7th baronet attained his majority in 1810. This proved to be a true prediction. It may be that the care of the house and estate was left entirely in the hands of the steward (John made several references to him in his letters), or that Sir William's stepbrother, the Reverend John Molesworth, the Rector of the nearby living of St Breock, was asked to hold a watching brief. Contemporary accounts record the Rector's success in improving his 'parsonage house' and garden, and we know of the interest shown by him in the course of a visit made by him to Pencarrow in 1806, but there is no record that Sir Arscott or any of his immediate family visited Pencarrow until

1812, after the 7th baronet had come of age and married. Even then, when Sir Arscott came on to Pencarrow from Tetcott, John Clift did not expect the family to stay long for 'the house is not yet furnish'd', and they would be forced to lodge temporarily at Costislost, a nearby farm on the estate. The family was more often 'in residence' in subsequent years, and there is an uncorroborated claim that the house underwent a 'complete repair' in the last three year of Sir Arscott' life[5], but there was another period of dormant non-occupancy after his death in 1823 until Sir William, 8th baronet, returned from his 'grand tour' on the continent to celebrate his coming of age in 1831.

Whoever had overall responsibility for Pencarrow house and the estate after the death of the 6th baronet, John Clift, according to his sister Elizabeth in a letter she wrote William in July 1799, was charged together with 'old Mr Rundell' and 'one man more' to 'look after the hous and to ceep it in repare'. No fire was to be lit in the house for a year, and John was apprehensive of the deterioration which he thought would inevitably ensue for already the house was looking very 'wisht' (i.e.dismal/wretched) with 'all the Plastering in the frunt falling down then'.

From entries in the estate accounts, we know that scaffolding and ropes were hired and the services of a 'plaisterer' engaged to enable the front of the house to be repaired in 1801; more scaffolding and ropes were paid for further repairs (perhaps as a result of the Revd John Molesworth's visit) in 1806 and 1807. We learn, too, that the house was cleaned by Mary Nutting for 4 shillings, the chimneys were swept at a cost of 17 shillings, the guttering repaired for £43.15s in 1798, and that Gideon Broad, a plumber and glazier, was paid £35.16s.10d in 1798, £4.16s.1d. in 1801 and £17.16s.2d in 1808 for work done in the house. There also a number of artisans (carpenters and masons in particular) whose names recur in the accounts, but it is not possible to be certain how much of the work for which they were paid was done elsewhere on the estate away from Pencarrow house. John Clift is a case in point for we know that he did work as a painter in Bodmin in 1793, in Tregonna and at St.Kew in 1798, but thereafter seems to have been employed solely at work at Pencarrow. However, together with George Bavin, Philip Hambly and Richard Greenwood, John Clift's name appears in the lists of each of the years for which accounts of this period survive. Like Clift, Philip Hambly was a carpenter (and it appears that his father before him was employed on the estate); Richard Greenwood was classed as a labourer but was obviously mainly employed as a 'hedger and ditcher,' and George Bavin was the gardener and it is the payments made to him which are remarkable.

		£	s	d
	Per contra Cr			
1801	Brought on	435	5	11
Nov.r 10th	Philip Hamley carpenter to this ins.t	3	14	2
	John Cliff do do	12	3	2
	J. Pollard Barge hire for Deals from Padstow		2	
12	Two Bush.l of corn for the House		15	
Dec.r 16	Richard Greenwood hedging p. Bill	13	19	4
	Bottles lost 6 Gallons of rum		7	6
23	John Jacob Mason p. Bill	5	5	
	John H. Genick p. Bill	2	15	1
	Thomas Reynolds do		10	10
29	Thomas Drury Taxes to Xmas	29	10	0
	Joseph George carpenter p. Bill	3	17	10
	John Dary do	1	5	6
	Gideon Broad p. Bill	4	16	1
30	Alex.r Mackinnick Lime Bill	6		
	Thomas Swoot Denabol quarry Stones p. Bill	14	16	2
31	David Rundall Smith do	6	17	10½
	John Ellery Mason do	6	7	10
	Philip Hamley carpenter do	4	11	2
	John Sloggot Mason do	10	10	2
	Robert Bestott do	3	2	5
	John Pollard p. Bill	10	0	5½
	Richard Greenwood do	2	10	10
	N. Norway & Son p. Bill	6	5	2
	Postage	2	17	4
		£506	9	0

A page from the Pencarrow estate accounts for November & December 1801

Over the eleven year period covered by the accounts George Bavin was paid in the region of £550 - approximately £130 in 1797, £223 in 1798, £35 in 1801, £51 in 1802, £52 in 1806 and £51 in 1808 - and the sum would undoubtedly be even greater if the accounts for the missing years were to surface. These amounts represent a very substantial outlay for the time and, while they obviously include Bavin's wages and money for specific projects (e.g. the new plantation at the head of the park in 1802), there must clearly have been considerable expense on plants, although there is only one mention of expenditure for them for an unspecified amount in 1806. Although Sir William, 8th baronet, is generally credited with the shaping and creation of the gardens of Pencarrow, it is clear that they were to be admired years before he undertook the remodelling in the 1830s and 1840s.

In 1826 Rudolph Ackermann wrote[6] on the basis of information gathered two years earlier by F.W.L.Stockdale during his *Excursions in the County of Cornwall,* that 'the park [at Pencarrow] contains some fine plantations' and 'much praise is due to Lady Molesworth[7] for many of the improvements, particularly in the grounds; also for the cultivation of many choice plants and shrubs. The gardens are very extensive, and most advantageously planned, with hot-houses, which produce as fine fruit as any place in the county.' Praise must also be given to George Bavin and to his successor Daniel Mackenzie for their gardening expertise.

Notes & References

1   The Clift Family Correspondence, 1792-1846, (ed.) Frances Austin, The Centre for English Cultural Tradition and Language, The University of Sheffield (1991). I would like to record my sincere gratitude to Dr Austin for her interest and helpful comments, and for generously allowing me to make extensive use of her research. Copies of her book are available for purchase in the Craft Gallery Shop at Pencarrow.
2   Cornwall County Record Office, Truro. Molesworth St Aubyn Papers, MA Box 48.
3   Add. Mss. 39955.
4   The Richard Owen Correspondence vols 7 and 8.
5   F.W.L.Stockdale, Excursions in the County of Cornwall, (London, 1824), p. 106.
6   R. Ackermann, The Repository of Arts, Literature, Fashion e/c.,vol.vii, (London, 1826), pp.126,127.
7   Lady Mary, widow of 7th baronet and mother of Sir William, 8th baronet.
    John Clift's letter (British Library Add. Mss. 39955, ff.95, 96) is reproduced by permission of the British Library.

The Mysterious Miss Dietz

The name of Harriet Jemima Dietz appears on the census returns of 1851 and 1861 for Pencarrow House/Mansion, and there are occasional tantalising references to her in the papers of Sir William[1] (1810-55) and the Reverend Sir Hugh Henry (1818-62), respectively the 8th & 9th Molesworth baronets. In both census returns she is described as a visitor to Pencarrow, unmarried and born c.1796 in Marylebone, London, and her death was recorded in Bodmin in the summer of 1862 her occupation was listed as 'gentlewoman', but in 1861 she had become a 'fundholder', confirming that she was of independent means. What is not clear is why she was a visitor to Pencarrow when there were no Molesworths in residence, and by what right or obligation did the Molesworth family allow her to stay at Pencarrow?

Alison Adburgham in her biography of Sir William quoted from a letter written by him to his sister Mary in June 1844 to support her presumption that Miss Dietz was a servant, more particularly, his wife-to-be Andalusia's personal maid. In the letter, Sir William, writing shortly before his marriage, bemoaned the fact that the restoration work to the mansion was not further forward and that Pencarrow was 'most uncomfortable, fit only for Miss Dietz and Ailsa, who concern themselves with killing the disturbed rats.' Miss Adburgham concluded that Harriet Dietz had been left in charge of the staff at Pencarrow to ensure that the mansion would be put the more quickly into a state fit to receive the newly wed baronet and his wife. It was a false conclusion, as Elizabeth Hawkins in 1841 and Rebecca McLean in 1851 and 1861 were listed in the census returns as the housekeepers at Pencarrow and, as will be shown, Harriet Dietz had figured in the Molesworth household for at least twenty years before the letter was written, long before Sir William met his future bride Andalusia Temple West.

The first mention I have come across of Harriet Dietz in the Molesworth archives is in another letter written by Sir William, on this occasion in June 1824, when he was barely fourteen years of age. He wrote to his mother to say, among other things, that 'I have left some books with Miss Dietz which I should like to have.' There are other references in Sir William's correspondence: writing to his sister Elizabeth in 1835, he asks her to remind Miss Dietz 'that she has forgot to send me the correspondence between the Colonial Office and the Governor of New South Wales,' and later that same year he wrote in a letter to his sister Mary, that he was 'excessively obliged to Miss Dietz for her cap' and, in 1844, in another letter to Mary he mentions a note he has received from Miss Dietz containing 'interesting accounts of rats and dogs and of dry rot [at Pencarrow].' In the same year he wrote to his mother asking her to buy a shawl for Miss Dietz – perhaps a gift by way of thanks to her for coping with the rats and other discomforts during the renovations at Pencarrow?

Clearly, Harriet Dietz was no servant, neither was she a member of the family, yet her social standing was such that it was not out of the ordinary for her to make up a 'partie carree' (foursome) in 1858 with a Lord in Waiting to Queen Victoria (Viscount Torrington), Andalusia, Lady Molesworth and the Revd. Hugh Molesworth. At the risk of making the same mistake as Miss Adburgham, I think Miss Dietz was what many a genteel young lady without connections and fortune became in the 19th century – a governess for Sir William's three sisters – Elizabeth, Catherine and Mary. There is evidence to support this claim for, Elizabeth, who died tragically young in 1836 at the age of twenty-four, left the sum of £146.15s.9d. in her will to pay for 'Miss Dietz's annuity.' That there was a close relationship between Miss Dietz and Elizabeth is borne out in a letter from Sir William to her in 1836, shortly before the latter's death:

'My dear Miss Dietz,
Accept from me a slight testimony of the Regard and respect which years of acquaintance have founded upon the firmest basis. I am glad to hear so favourable an account of Elizabeth. I must, however, deprecate strongly her exciting herself in any way. I beseech you to keep her quiet. Believe me,
Yours affectionately,
William Molesworth.'

Sir William Molesworth died in 1855 and, by the terms of his will, his widow and then his sister Mary had the right to reside in the mansion of Pencarrow during their lifetime. Andalusia lived until 1888, surviving her husband by some thirty-three years, and Mary, who had married Richard Ford in 1851 and was widowed in 1858, did not die until 1910, consequently the Reverend Sir Hugh Henry Molesworth, who succeeded his cousin as the 9th baronet but died in 1862, never lived at Pencarrow. Nevertheless, he lived not far away in Little Petherick near Padstow (where he was Rector of the church of St Petroc Minor), was a frequent visitor and guest of Andalusia, and he invariably called on Miss Dietz on his visits to Pencarrow even when Andalusia was not in residence. Thus he recorded in his diaries[2] not only visiting her at Pencarrow (14 Nov. and 13 Dec. 1856; 16 Jan., 30 Jan., 25 Apr., 17 Aug. and 8 Oct. 1857; 19 Mar., 1 April, 6 May 1858; 29 Mar. 1859; 14 Jun., 9 Dec. 1861), but also calling on her in London when he was on a visit there in June 1860. Moreover, he intriguingly recorded calling on Miss Dietz 'in her cottage' on 6 May 1858. We also know from a letter which he wrote to Mary Ford that Harriet Dietz suffered an illness in April/May 1861 which laid her low for more than six weeks.

Further confirmation of her privileged status vis-à-vis the Molesworth family was the fact that she appears in the 1841 census in the return made for the rectory at St. Breock, the residence of the Revd. William Molesworth (Sir William's uncle), his second wife Frances, their younger son, Paul (later, in 1862, to become the 10th Molesworth baronet) and their daughter, Frances, then ten years old. Harriet Dietz is listed as a visitor and 'independent.' At about this time, it emerges from a letter written in 1842 by Sir William to his solicitor and trustee, that he had promised to provide a house for her. He wrote:

'My dear Woollcombe,
.......I promised Miss Dietz one [cottage] like those built last, one of which she was to have had. I grudge building ornamental cottages when I don't want them, and especially at the present moment when I am so hard up for cash. In looking at my estimates, I see that I have put down £600 for repairs of Mansion & premises & for farm buildings this year – this sum must not be exceeded on any account, and I think not more than £150 can be allowed out of it for a cottage. I will do what I promised, but nothing more. If Miss Dietz chooses to live at Dunmere, then it would be worth while to expend an extra hundred or one hundred & fifty pounds, but not on a useless cottage at the {hut downs}[3] ' I don't believe Miss Dietz will ever continue to live at either of the two places, & I think it is an entirely foolish fancy. I am most happy to make her a gift of the £150 (for as to my taking any rent for the cottage, that I could not think of doing), but I want to do nothing more.....'

£150 in those days was a substantial sum (see note 4 below) and for Sir William to contemplate spending 25% of the money he had allocated for his building/repair fund for 1842 on accommodation for Harriet Dietz with no intention of charging rent subsequently is surely a measure of her standing with him and in the Molesworth family. We know that the cottage that became hers was Ailsa cottage in the Pencarrow estate (now Shepherd's Hill on the Bodmin-Wadebridge road between Maryland and Sladesbridge), which must have been built in the early 1840s. If any additional evidence of Harriet Dietz's gentility and social standing is needed it comes in the following unsigned and undated but charming letter which she wrote to Sir Hugh Henry Molesworth in 1856 on hearing of his engagement and forthcoming marriage to the daughter of another leading family in north

Cornwall, the Prideaux Brune of Place, Padstow, with whose family Harriet Dietz was also clearly familiar:

'My dear Sir Hugh,
I congratulate you and all who love you – especially myself – that you are to marry a granddaughter of the late Mrs Prideaux Brune [5] who captivated me as few have done, as she united the charms of ladylike manners to the superior and more uncommon ones of Christian feeling. I therefore trust the Almighty will bless your future life with as much happiness as it is possible to enjoy in our present state of existence, and I am already anticipating the pleasure I shall have whenever you both pass Ailsa Cottage. Pray present my best regards and congratulations to Mrs [6] and Miss Molesworth [7] [&] my best love to your sister [8] who must be delighted to have her old friend mistress of Little Petherick.'

Only some of the mystery has been solved, however. We may have rightly deduced that she was a governess, but we don't know for instance how, when or where Miss Dietz and the Molesworth family made contact or whether the Ailsa of 1844 who killed rats was the dog after whom Harriet's cottage was named? Nevertheless, we can be in no doubt that she was someone held in high regard by the Molesworth family and someone for whom they made Pencarrow a home for many years after her primary function vis-à-vis the family had been successfully fulfilled.

'Miss Dietz and the Galley Slaves'

Of one thing, however, we may be sure, and that is that Harriet Jemima Dietz and dogs had a very close association as is affection-ately illustrated in this pen and ink sketch in the Pencarrow visitors' book.[9]

Notes & References

1   *A Radical Aristocrat,* (Padstow, 1990), pp. 84, 85.
2   Sadly the only diaries which have been discovered cover only the years between his marriage in 1856 his death in January 1862.
3   The writing is not very legible and the location cannot be identified.
4   The equivalent sum today would be c£7,200!
5   Frances, wife of the Revd Charles Prideaux (Prideaux Brune after 1799). She died in 1831.
6   Frances Molesworth (neé Buller), Sir Hugh's stepmother.
7   His aunt Caroline Molesworth (1794-1872).
8   Frances Molesworth.
9   c.1859, possibly by Edward Underdown.

Mary Ford's 'People' at Pencarrow 1888 - 1910

The last Will and Testament of Sir William Molesworth who died in 1855 stipulated that his widow, Andalusia, and then his sister, Mary, 'shall be at liberty to reside in my Mansion House of Pencarrow' during their lifetime, and they were also empowered by the Will to 'decide whether the Hothouses, Greenhouses, Stables, Ornamental Gardens and Pleasure Grounds shall or shall not be kept up or restored.' Andalusia outlived her husband by thirty-three years, leaving Mary, by then the widow of Richard Ford for thirty years, the chatelaine of the family seat from 1888 until she died in 1910, in her ninety-fifth year.

Neither Andalusia nor Mary Ford made Pencarrow their principal residence, preferring to retain their London houses, but both chose to preserve and maintain the garden amenities and features created by Sir William. Both chatelaines spent some weeks at a time at Pencarrow, Andalusia coming invariably at the end of the London season in the late summer and early autumn, when she hosted house parties which attracted leading members of the capital's beau monde to Cornwall. But, while these visits did not take place every year (she did not come to Pencarrow from 1868-74, 1879-82 nor from 1884-88), Mary Ford divided her time more evenly and regularly between London and Pencarrow each year from the first summer of her tenancy in 1888, until she died at Pencarrow. For Andalusia a visit to Pencarrow was a diverting rural interlude, for Mary Ford it was a homecoming - a difference in attitude which explains why Andalusia only grudgingly agreed to supplement from the money she had inherited from her husband the income from the estate when it fell short of what was needed for the upkeep of the house and garden, whereas Mary willingly provided funds for not only the necessary maintenance, but also, for initiatives in the gardens and pleasure grounds. Moreover, while Andalusia exhibited a benevolent, but transient interest in her workforce at Pencarrow, Mary Ford's attitude and conduct illustrated the true meaning of noblesse oblige at work on her employees, whom she was fond of calling 'my people.'

The records of Mary Ford's 'people' are far from complete. We know that when she was not in residence, the household staff was limited to a housekeeper, a cook and a maid. The housekeeper in 1888 was Elizabeth Wright and she was succeeded sometime in the 1890s by Mary Creber who was made redundant (with an ex gratia of £20) by Sir Lewis Molesworth after Mary's death in 1910. Census returns reveal Ann Garland (1881) and

Eden Pendray (1891) as the cooks; the housemaids were Agnes Garland (1881), Martha Morrish (1891) and Eva Lobb (1901) who, like Mary Creber, was deemed surplus to requirements after Mary Ford's death. Also, when Mary came to Pencarrow each year she brought her London household with her which consisted of a butler, footman/page, cook, lady's maid and a housemaid. At the time of her death at Pencarrow, the butler was William Thorogood, the cook was Mrs Gordon, Miss Newton was the lady's maid, there were two footmen, W.Price & W.Fisk, and a coachman, W. Rolf. From the list of attendants at Mary Ford's funeral; it is possible Miss E.L.Gill and Miss E.Gill were also part of the household staff. We have no idea of the wages earned by the domestic staff, nor of their conditions of employment.

Back row: Cleave Wedge, Tom Biddick, Bill Masters, Frank Yelland, Hedley Lobb, Sam Craddock, Arthur Hoskins, jnr.
Middle Row: Jim Hoskin, Jim Beare, Sid Clemens, John Hoskin, Bill Carter, Alfred Bate, George Hoskin, John Cox, John Gill, jnr., Will Abbott.
Front row: Francis Stevenson, John Dyer, Jack Hosken, Bill Craddock, Richard Meager, William Bate, Frank Abbott, Charles Hoskin, Arthur Hosking, snr., John Gill, snr., Aubrey Bartlett, snr., (Howard Bartlett, aged 6?)
The original photograph (1905) is in the possession of John Borrott, the grandson of John Gill (Snr) & names were put to faces in the 1950s by Arthur Hosking (Jnr), the last survivor of those photographed.

Maintenance & Woodmen Regularly Employed (1888 - 1911) and their Daily Rates of Pay																											
Name	Born	Trade	88	89	90	91	92	93	94	95	96	97	98	99	0	1	2	3	4	5	6	7	8	9	10	11
Stevenson F.G.	1860	Foreman	*	*	*	*	*	*	*	*	(5/-	*	*	*	*	*	*	*	*	*	*	*	*	*	*	*
Abbott Ernest	1886																2/2	*	*	2/4	2/6	*	3/-			
Abbott Frank	1844					3'	*	*	*	*	*	*	*	*	*	*	*	*	*	*						
Abbott Sidney	1878												1/8												
Abbott William	1867		*																							
Bate Alfred	1874		1/8	*	*	*	*	*	*	2/-	*	2/2	2/6	*	*	*	*	*	*	*	*	*	*	*	*	*
Bate William	1842		2/4	*	*	*	*	*	*	*	*	*	2/6	*	*	*	*	*	*	*	*	*				
Beare Jeremiah	1860								2/-				2/6										*			
Beare Silas	1845							2/-	*	*																
Carhart Joseph							3/6	*	*			*														
Carhart Thomas	1857																						2/9	*	*	*
Carter William	1861					2/4	*	*	*	*	*	*	2/6	*	*	*	*	*	*	*	*	*	*	*	*	*
Cocks J.																	2/6	*	*	*	*	*	*	*	*
Craddock Sam	1875	Sawyer							*	*			*	*	*	*	*	*	*	*	*	*	*	*	*	*
Craddock Wm	1844	Sawyer	*	*	*	*	*	*	*	*	*	*	*	*	*	*	*	*	*	*	*	*	*	*	*	*
Dyer John	1846					2/4	*	*	*	*							2/6	*	*	*	*	*	*	*	*	*
Ellery Isaiah	1822	Mason	*	*	*	*																				
Gill John	1856	Mason					*	*	*	*	*	*	*	*	*	*	*	*	*	*	*	*	*	*	*	*
Hosken Geo.	1867		2/2	*	*	*	*	*	*	*	2/4	*	2/6	*	*	*	*	*	*	*	*	*	*	*	*	*
Hoskin Hart	1850	Carpenter	*	*	*	*	*	*	*	*	*	*	*	*	*	*	*	*	*	*	*	*	*	*	*	*
Hosken James				*	*	*	2/4	*	*	*			*	*	*	*	*	*	*	*	*					
Hoskin William	1819		1/4	*	*	*	1/6																			
Lightfoot Tom	1831								2/4	*	*	*	2/6	*	*	*	*	*	*	*	*	*	*	*		
Meagor Richd.	1832		2/4	*	*	*	*	*	*	*	*	*	2/6	*	*	*	*	*	*	*						
Osborne John	1846					4/2		2/6	*										*		*	*		3/-		
Scott Elijah	1848	Mason						*	*	*	*	*	*	*	*	*	*	*	*	*	*	*	*	*	*	*

The master masons & carpenter employed their own labourers & submitted their accounts which were paid by Stevenson at the end of each month. Details are known only of John Gill's workmmen.

Gill remained employed until 1926 and E.Wills until 1921.

Name	Trade	88	89	90	91	92	93	94	95	96	97	98	99	0	1	2	3	4	5	6	7	8	9	10	11
F.Cleave	Labourer															*	*	*							
John Gill (jnr)	Labourer															*	*	*	*	*	*	*	*		
F. Gill	Labourer																		*	*	*	*	*	*	
E. Wills	Labourer															*	*	*	*	*	*	*	*	*	

Information gleaned from John Gill's accounts ledger in the possession of his grandson John Borrott.

We have more, but still incomplete, information about the Mary Ford's outdoor employees. The head gardener when she inherited Pencarrow was Henry Jones; he was succeeded in 1898 by Aubrey Bartlett who was still 'in post' in 1910. Frank and then Ernest Abbott were the head gamekeepers, and the estate foreman from 1888 was Francis Stevenson. Regrettably, the records of the head gardeners and the gamekeepers have not survived, but

Stevenson's annual account books are a mine of information, and form the basis of the table of maintenance/woodmen regularly employed at Pencarrow 1888-1911. There is also a picture of some of the outside staff photographed in front of the hothouses which ranged along the edge of the east lawn, where the long wisteria border is now to be found.

Stevenson recorded payments to more than fifty other workmen in Mary Ford's time, but they were employed either on a temporary very short-term basis or to undertake a specific task – e.g. the Hambly brothers, James and Joe, excavating for water pipes and digging wells in the 1900s.

A comparison between the table and those named in the photograph reveal discrepancies and anomalies. Aubrey Bartlett, the head gardener, and Frank Abbott, gamekeeper, appear in the photograph, but their wages were not paid by the estate foreman; they were sufficiently independent to be answerable for their expenses directly to the Trustees of the Pencarrow Estate, who paid their wages from a separate account. It must be assumed that the men who appear in the photograph, but who are not mentioned in the table - Jim Beare, Tom Biddick, Sid Clemens, Charles Hosken, George Hosken, Jim Hosken, Arthur Hosking (Snr & Jnr), Hedley Lobb, Bill Masters, Cleave Wedge and Frank Yelland - were gardeners, and not the retainers that were Stevenson's immediate responsibility and who were described by Mary Ford as her 'Carpenters and Weedmen.' As for anomalies, it is virtually impossible to distinguish between the various Hoskens/Hoskings/Hoskins – these surnames are spelled capriciously both in Stevenson's account books and in the 1891 and 1901 census returns, and there is no way of telling which is appropriate in a particular setting: John Cox in the photograph was presumably the J. Cocks in the table; and was Jeremiah Beare also Jim Beare, and was he related to the various members of the family surnamed Bear also mentioned in the accounts?

The master masons and master carpenter were paid monthly in arrears by the estate foreman after submitting a detailed account of the expenses incurred and the labour involved in the work the master and his 'gang', had undertaken at Pencarrow or at any of the many properties on the estate. As shown in the table, the wages of the estate workmen were calculated on a daily basis and paid weekly. Francis Stevenson was engaged @ 4/2d per diem in 1888, rising to 5/- in 1896. All those in his charge were paid according to age - Alfred Bate (Jnr) earned 1/4d aged 14 in 1888, but was earning 2/6d ten years later - and ability/experience were rewarded with wage increases as competence increased. Some, like the thatchers (Henry Ash, J[ohn] Old and the Carharts) were paid on the basis of piece-work; the sawyers, Craddock father and son, were paid by the foot for the amount of wood sawn (they earned more for sawing hardwood (oak) than soft wood (fir); John Dyer and George Hoskin were sometimes paid on a contract to break stones, or to fell trees and make faggots in Dunmere wood, and James and Joe Hambly were brought in to dig wells and lay pipes Men worked six days in the week (Christmas Day included) and, if holidays or days off work were taken, it was without pay. There is some evidence, however, that long and loyal service was rewarded not only with a personal gift from Mary Ford, but also with an annuity or a pension, and sick pay was not out of the question. Elijah Scott, the master mason responsible for work on the Molesworth estate properties in the St Mabyn/St.Kew areas suffered an accident at work in 1906 and was allowed 15/- a week for the three weeks during which he could not work.

There was usually a clear division in the work undertaken by the masons, carpenters and their 'gangs'. The former coped with minor building works, sweeping chimneys, cementing, plastering, paving, walling, laying drains, whereas the carpenters made and mended doors, windows, fences and gates, as well as glazing, and interior decorating. However, there were jobs for which no special skill was required, which were tackled by anyone and everyone working on the estate. Anyone could be expected to be called upon to lend a hand with the annual spring-clean in the house (moving furniture and beating carpets), to help with 'brushing' (acting as beaters) for the Pencarrow shoots, snow clearance, harvesting, hedging, whitewashing walls, cleaning carriages, lopping trees, cutting weeds in the gardens, charcoal burning in Dunmere wood, hoeing and cutting off 'mangolds'(sic) and, in 1889, even helping with the 'mackadamizing'(sic) of the drive.

The wages paid to the estate workers were not ungenerous for the time, and most of the men lived with their families in Molesworth-owned properties at a reasonable rent. John Gill and his family lived at Pencarrow Mill at an annual rent of £6: Frank Abbott was charged £5.10s rent for Ivy Cottage. The rent for the cottages at Maryland was £4pa, but Silas Beare and his family lived in a cottage in Sladesbridge for as little as £2.50pa. Curiously, Aubrey Bartlett was charged only £4pa for the rent of the Gardener's Cottage at Pencarrow but, presumably this was a reduced rent and a perquisite of his position as head gardener.

In the second half of the first decade of the century, Francis Stevenson hosted early in the year a 'Tradesman's Supper' provided by Mrs Eleanor Pollard, the landlady of The Molesworth Arms in Wadebridge. Usually about 45 men attended and ate suppers @ 2/6d. per head. In 1907,

Stevenson also paid for 2 decanters of brandy, 'grog' to the value of £2.16s.4d., 1/- worth of tobacco and 4/- for the hire of a piano – a total expense of £8.16s.4d. In the next three years he paid out £9.2s, £9.6s.9d and £8.7s.6d. respectively. In 1910, he noted an additional expense of 10/- for 'whiskey' for the visitors. No attendance list or guest list has survived for any of the suppers, and we don't know who made up the tradesmen or the visitors, but it would be a confirmation of the generosity and beneficence characteristic of Mary Ford that at least some of her 'Gardeners, Gamekeepers, Carpenters and Weedmen' – her 'people' as she loved to call her employees were there deservedly to enjoy what was undoubtedly a merry and jovial celebration.

Mary Ford's bookplate

The Gardens of Pencarrow before 1830

The renown of the gardens at Pencarrow dates from the initiatives and innovations introduced by Sir William Molesworth, 8th baronet, in the twenty or so years following his return in 1831 from a 'grand tour' through Germany, France and particularly Italy, until his untimely death at the age of forty-five in 1855. But, what of the gardens before 1830? No definitive written or artistic description of their extent, design or content has survived, but this paper is an attempt to piece together the very few clues and references which have been found in the Pencarrow archive.

Much of the lay-out of the gardens as we know them today still bear Sir William's imprint and, thanks to the meticulous records to be found in his Garden Book (still preserved at Pencarrow), we know not only what he landscaped, but also what he planted, when he planted and where he planted. Further planting details were provided by Sir William's sister, Mrs Mary Ford, to whom Pencarrow passed on the death of Sir William's widow, Andalusia, in 1888. The list of trees was revised and updated in 1928 when Sir Hugh Molesworth-St. Aubyn, 13th baronet, instigated further planting, and his son, Sir John, subsequently planted many of the colourful shrubs still seen today. However, the most significant twentieth century contribution was made by the 15th baronet, Lt. Col. Sir Arscott Molesworth-St. Aubyn who, together with his wife, Iona, restored the gardens after the dereliction they had suffered during and after the Second World War. In 1978, Sir Arscott again updated the list of trees in the gardens, replaced many of the tree casualties and, by 1991, had planted more than 160 different species of specimen conifers together with some 570 different species and hybrids of rhododendron, and more than 60 different camellias. Consequently, while it is not difficult to trace in some detail the development of the 'modern' (i.e. post 1830) gardens, the virtual non-existence of relevant records before the second quarter of the nineteenth century makes it a challenging task to speculate upon the shape and contents of the grounds and gardens of Pencarrow before Sir William launched his alterations and innovations.

The legal records cited by Sir John Maclean in his account of the manor of Pencarrow reveal that it was acquired by the Molesworth family in two stages. The manor does not appear in Saxton's 1576 map of Cornwall, but in 1603, John Molesworth, his wife Catherine and eldest son Hender were granted a moiety of the Manor, comprising 'one messuage [house and outbuildings], one barn, one garden, two orchards, 50 acres of land, 10 acres of meadow, 60 acres of pasture and 80 acres of brambles and briars,' and in 1626 Hender Molesworth purchased for £400 the remainder of the Manor - the 'capital messuage, farm, barton and demesne lands [all freehold land and houses] called Pencarrow.'

The 'capital messuage' of Pencarrow is thought to have stood on the site of the present mansion, but of the garden there is no longer any trace of what might have existed as an Elizabethan or Stuart model, the pattern of which usually featured a knot garden close to the house with the parterres enclosed by raised walks bordered by low hedges. By 1650, the name 'Mowsworth'(sic) appeared as a landowner at 'Egloshale'(sic) on John Norden's map of the Trigg Hundred in Cornwall, but there is no mention of Pencarrow, even though there is space enough. Neither the house nor estate gave rise to any recorded comment for the rest of the century, but Thomas Tonkin was impressed c.1700 by the 'beautiful house' which Sir John Molesworth, 2nd baronet was building with the 'bright clear freestone' from a quarry on the estate. Tonkin mentions that the lands of the barton of Pencarrow were fruitful, rich in wood, water and stone, but he makes no mention of a garden.

Until the nineteenth century, Pencarrow did not attract visits from any of the inquisitive and curious travellers who came to Cornwall and later described their itinerary. For example Celia Fiennes did not make a detour from her route from Wadebridge to Camelford in 1695; Daniel Defoe who made a tour in Devon and Cornwall in 1724 mentioned Lanhydrock, but not Pencarrow; John Loveday, scholar and antiquary, made a series of summer tours around Britain one of which, in 1736, was to the West Country and Cornwall. En route from Camelford to Bodmin he and his party went out of their way to visit Lanhydrock (which they found to be 'extremely out of repair') but not Pencarrow, which would have involved even less of a detour from their route. The Revd. Dr Richard Pococke did visit Pencarrow in 1750, but limited his comments to the dimensions of the 'ancient camp' in the grounds. Pencarrow was not worthy of a mention by Dr William Maton, botanist and geologist, on his travels (1794-6) and, while James Forbes waxed lyrical about the scenery of the 'varied vale of Egloshayle', Pencarrow held no attraction for him, for he left the house 'at some distance' on his way from Wadebridge to Bodmin in 1794.

The only other pre-1830 references to Pencarrow described, as Dr Pococke did, the very impressive 'Pencarrow Rounds' – the Iron Age earth-works on the estate to the south of the mansion – but, otherwise, mentioned only that there was a deer park in the grounds. William Borlase writing in 1758 mentioned Pencarrow as one of eleven such parks in Cornwall, as did Samuel and Daniel Lysons in 1814, by which time the county's deer parks had dwindled to nine in number, but neither source gave any indication of the exact location, the extent of the park or whether it was enclosed by a ditch or a fence. By 1824, however, Pencarrow is not included in a list of deer parks listed in the county by Hutchins and Drew in their *History of Cornwall*.

The 'capital messuage' of Pencarrow which Hender Molesworth purchased in 1626 was, in all probability, an Elizabethan/Jacobean manor house of which there is little or no trace today. It is reasonable to assume that the garden design would also be reshaped on the occasions when the house was adapted or modernized during the next 200 years. It has not been possible to pinpoint the exact dates when significant changes were made to the house and, consequently, when changes might have been made in the garden, and what indications there are, are tantalisingly imprecise.

Hender Molesworth died in 1647, and it is not known whether his elder son, also named Hender (1628-89), ever resided at Pencarrow after his father's death. It is known he was at one time a factor of the Royal Africa Company and had settled in Jamaica by 1666, where he acquired an estate of more than 6,000 acres. He served as acting Governor of the island for a period in the reign of James II and, in July 1689, he had the distinction of being the first baronet created by the new king, William III, in recognition of his loyal service in Jamaica to the protestant crown. He returned to England in the same year, where he died and was buried in London barely two months after he had been created a baronet, but there is no evidence to suggest that he came to Pencarrow in 1689 or at any other time after he had settled in Jamaica.

Hender died childless and his younger brother, John (1635-1716) who succeeded to the newly created baronetcy, and who had been knighted by Charles II in 1675 for services in Cornwall, was indisputably 'in residence' at Pencarrow before 1700 since, as already mentioned, Tonkin wrote at that time of 'the beautiful house' which the second baronet 'has not yet quite finished'. If Sir John Molesworth's intention was to follow the latest trend in garden design, he would have introduced a flat, level garden with clipped hedges, topiary and symmetrically-shaped flower beds, very much along the lines of what is known to have existed in the last decade of the seventeenth century at nearby Lanhydrock and at Prideaux Place in

Padstow early in the eighteenth century but, if they were introduced, no trace has survived. Furthermore, if Sir John had wished to be in the vanguard of innovators in respect of the planting of his garden, he was well-placed, since he had not only inherited his brother's baronetcy but also his estate in Jamaica. This inheritance could have supplied him with a range of the exotic flowers, plants and trees from the Caribbean and West Indies which were becoming increasingly in vogue in England at the turn of the seventeenth and eighteenth centuries. Some of these exotics could have been grown out of doors, but the more tender plants would have needed the protection of an early greenhouse or stove house of the sort first known to have existed in the reign of William and Mary. If the second Molesworth baronet had been such a garden enthusiast and pioneered the cultivation of exotics in Cornwall, it is inconceivable that Tonkin would not have remarked upon his horticultural initiatives. Consequently, with no corroborative contemporary evidence and certainly no traces to be found in the gardens, it must be assumed that Sir John was preoccupied with his house and not the gardens.

There are two further references to the reconstruction of Pencarrow in the eighteenth century. The Lysons brothers referred to the mansion being built in the year 1730, and quote William Borlase who described it as 'perhaps the most capacious mansion in Cornwall'. They offer no corroboration of this statement, but another source suggests that some changes might have been taking place in the garden, if not at the house, at about that time. In 1730, Robert Furber, a gardener with a nursery at Kensington Park Gate in London, published what is generally thought to have been the first nurseryman's catalogue entitled *Twelve Months of Flowers*, which consisted of twelve plates, one for each month of the year, of appropriate flower arrangements of hand-coloured engravings by Henry Fletcher of paintings by the Dutch artist, Pieter Casteels. As John Harvey, a noted horticultural historian, has pointed out, the plants which were depicted were principally florists' flowers – auricula, anemone, hyacinth, rose – but there were also some two dozen 'exotic' plants from America. The plants were all numbered and were identifiable by a key at the foot of the plate. A thirteenth plate was produced with a dedication to The Prince of Wales and the Princess Royal which carried within a floral border a list of more than 430 subscribers to the catalogue, among whom are to be found the names of Lady Molesworth, Lady St. Aubyn and the Thomas Herbert, Earl of Pembroke.

The significance of a link between these aristocrats in the development of garden design in the West Country can best be illustrated by the following diagram in which the estates with which they were associated are named and highlighted:

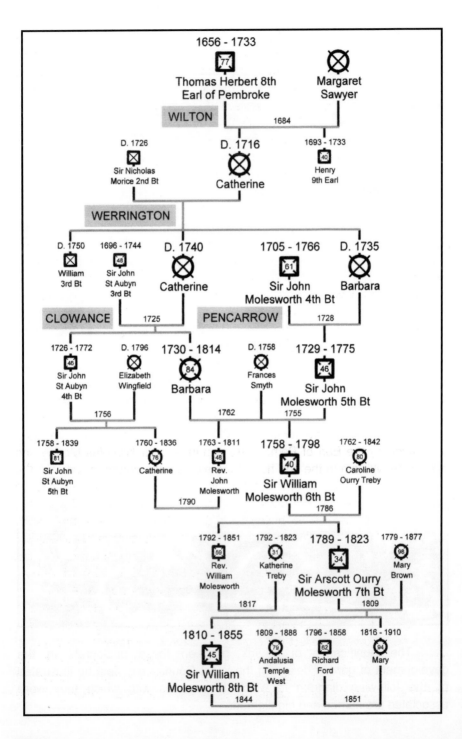

1656 - 1733
77
Thomas Herbert 8th
Earl of Pembroke

Margaret
Sawyer

WILTON

1684

D. 1726
Sir Nicholas
Morice 2nd Bt

D. 1716
Catherine

1693 - 1733
40
Henry
9th Earl

WERRINGTON

D. 1750
William
3rd Bt

1696 - 1744
48
Sir John
St Aubyn
3rd Bt

D. 1740
Catherine

1705 - 1766
61
Sir John
Molesworth 4th Bt

D. 1735
Barbara

CLOWANCE

1725

PENCARROW

1728

1726 - 1772
46
Sir John
St Aubyn
4th Bt

D. 1796
Elizabeth
Wingfield

1730 - 1814
84
Barbara

D. 1758
Frances
Smyth

1729 - 1775
46
Sir John
Molesworth 5th Bt

1756

1762

1755

1758 - 1839
81
Sir John
St Aubyn
5th Bt

1760 - 1836
75
Catherine

1763 - 1811
48
Rev.
John
Molesworth

1758 - 1798
40
Sir William
Molesworth 6th Bt

1762 - 1842
80
Caroline
Ourry Treby

1790

1786

1792 - 1851
59
Rev.
William
Molesworth

1792 - 1823
31
Katherine
Treby

1789 - 1823
34
Sir Arscott Ourry
Molesworth 7th Bt

1779 - 1877
98
Mary
Brown

1817

1809

1810 - 1855
45
Sir William
Molesworth 8th Bt

1809 - 1888
79
Andalusia
Temple
West

1796 - 1858
82
Richard
Ford

1816 - 1910
94
Mary

1844

1851

It should be pointed out that, at the time of the publication of Furber's catalogue, there were two Lady Molesworths alive – Barbara, the wife of Sir John Molesworth, the 4th baronet, and Jane, married to Richard, the head of another branch of the Molesworth family for whom a viscountcy had been created in 1719, and who had succeeded his elder brother John as the 3rd Viscount Molesworth of Swords in 1726. The 1st and 2nd viscounts were known to have been keen gardeners, but the wife of the 3rd viscount was not the subscriber listed by Furber. All those named appeared in strict order of precedence under the appropriate letter of the alphabet, and the Lady Molesworth listed does not appear after Viscount Middleton and before Lord Malton (a baron), but is sandwiched between Lady Maynard and Lady Monson, each of whom, like her, was the wife of a baronet.

Nevertheless, for all their common interest in flowers, the Herbert family's influence on the eighteenth century changes effected in the gardens highlighted above lay principally, as it did elsewhere in the great estates of the land at that time, in landscaping and tree-planting. At Wilton, Isaac de Caus's formal renaissance garden, which had been designed to complement the seventeenth century Palladian house designed by Inigo Jones, was modified and simplified successively by the 8th earl, (a contemporary of the second and third Molesworth baronets), and his son 'the architect earl' who inherited Wilton in 1737. The changes brought about a more open landscape with picturesque vistas, the creation of a lake and a Palladian bridge together with more shrubberies and trees to augment the flower garden near the house. At Werrington, the landscape changes introduced by the Earl of Pembroke's son-in-law, Sir Nicholas Morice and his son Sir William in the first half of the eighteenth century, owed much to the influence of Sir Nicholas's wife's family, and also to William Kent and his advocacy of the natural style of landscaping which, prompted the introduction of ornamental buildings and structures to grace the vistas, terraces and walks. At Clowance, too, the Herbert influence is to be seen for the 9th earl of Pembroke is known to have designed at least the south front of the house for his niece Catherine and her husband, Sir John St. Aubyn. Subsequently, the parkland and pleasure gardens were developed and walks with vistas opened out in the grounds which Sir John had started to plant when he inherited the estate on the death of his father in 1723. All the above developments reflect the change in garden design whereby the rigid geometrical layout of the previous century was gradually replaced in the eighteenth century by more open and natural landscaping – a feature of which was that the park came up to the house, often leading to the disappearance of flower beds in front of the house.

When Barbara Morice married Sir John Molesworth in 1728, she will have brought with her not only her Herbert family interest in gardens and gardening, but also the money to finance any restructuring/replanting under consideration at Pencarrow. In addition to her settled portion of £6,000, she had inherited £4,000 on the death of her father in 1726 and was to inherit a further £2,000 in 1729 on the birth of her first child, John, later to succeed as the 5th Molesworth baronet. Unlike Wilton, Werrington and Clowance there is no record that any money was spent on the Pencarrow grounds/gardens at that time, and Lady Barbara left no lasting impression there before her untimely death in 1735.

After her death, Sir John was much preoccupied with parliamentary duties representing first Newport, and then the Duchy as a knight of the shire until 1761. At the time of his death in 1766, he had started upon the redevelopment of the mansion at Pencarrow which was completed by his son Sir John, the 6th baronet, but there are no plans of the house recon-struction, and we have no idea what was planned for the garden. Con-sequently, apart from attention being drawn to the pre-historic earthworks, the only eighteenth century references relating to the grounds of Pencarrow were made, as mentioned earlier, by William Borlase in 1758 and by the Lysons brothers in 1814, and they merely record the existence of a deer park, for which there is possibly some supporting evidence, even today. Fortunately, there is some pictorial evidence of the lay-out of part of the grounds in the second half of the eighteenth century.

There is in the Pencarrow collection of paintings a water-colour of the landscape immediately to the south of the house. The painting is unsigned and undated, but both its style and composition suggest that it was painted c.1770. Although the trees which are depicted (particularly the plantation in the middle ground to the right in the painting in line with the then front of the house) no longer feature in the modern garden, the contours of the land in the foreground are still recognizable. However, what is particularly striking is the only evidence that there was once a pond beyond the lawn in front of the house, on the house side of the tree plantation in the painting. Perspective makes it difficult to identify the source of the water, but the pond's outline and dimensions, clearly with no pretence to be a lake or even to be taken as an example of the sort of landscape water feature so much in vogue at that time are, nevertheless, rather greater than those associated with a dew pond. The pond had disappeared by the time the 8th baronet created the Italian garden in the 1830s – his sister Mary, who witnessed and later described the alterations, made no mention of its existence – but it is legitimate to wonder whether the fountain sited in the centre of the garden was placed there because of a ready source of water. It is also possible to make out a palisade in front of the house, and another stretching from the left of the picture and running below the shepherd and his sheep in the middle foreground. It should be pointed out, however, that landscape gardeners in the eighteenth century were quite as likely to create artistic impressions of their proposals as they were of drawing up plans of the finished work, and it may be that the painting in question was the landscape proposed, rather than the landscape completed but, what evidence there is, points to the picture having been painted from nature.

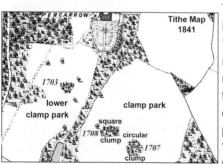

The tithe map of 1841 shows fields known as 'Lower Clamp Park', 'Circular Clump' and 'Square Clump', numbered 1703, 1707 and 1708 respectively on the map. Area 1707, the Circular Clump is just where the circular plantation is sited in the painting. The planting of trees in 'clumps' or groves was a feature of the parkland of the eighteenth century and quite in keeping with deer being enclosed therein. In 1820, C.S.Gilbert described the deer park at Pencarrow as being 'dotted over with firs and other straggling trees, and skirted with umbrageous woods which form, in the distance, a diversity of pleasing swells'. This is a description which rings true today, even if there are cattle grazing in the park, and not deer. A pencil sketch Pencarrow mansion made, c.1812, by Mary Molesworth, the wife of the 7th baronet, and an 1824 engraving by F.W.L. Stockdale of the south front of the house show the lawn (remembered as an 'exceedingly ugly lawn' by Mary Ford in 1900) coming right up to the house.

The part of the lawn nearest the house appears to be enclosed to the south by a palisade which is so insubstantial that it is clearly intended to be more of an ornamental boundary than a deterrent to wandering deer – if indeed there ever were deer at Pencarrow, for neither Borlase, Lysons nor Gilbert mention any fauna. It may be that the Molesworths, like other landowners in the eighteenth century created the park merely to enjoy a picturesque landscape 'prospect', a feature so much sought after in the estates of that period, and the palisade may have been installed to corral sheep used to crop the grass and prevent them from coming too close to the house. The south lawn was converted into a garden in the Italian style by the 8th baronet in the 1830s, but some 'clumps' in the park can still be recognised today, and Charles Henderson, the twentieth century Cornish historian, clearly believed in the existence of a deer park. When he visited Pencarrow in the 1920s, Henderson identified 'old stone palings of the park sticking out of the top of the earth bank or hedge, west of the main drive'

At this point, it is perhaps relevant to recall that Pencarrow was not the only country estate which the Molesworth family owned in the eighteenth century. On the death of John Arscott in 1788, his family's estate at Tetcott, near Holsworthy in North Devon, was inherited by Sir William Molesworth as a consequence of his great-grandfather's marriage to Jane Arscott some ninety years earlier. Drawings made of Tetcott house in c.1809 reveal that it was a more substantial building than the mansion at Pencarrow but, in common with the family seat in Cornwall at that time, there are no flower beds visible and the park goes right up to the house, cut only by the sweep of the entrance drive.

Tetcott House

The Molesworths, in common with most of the landed gentry in the eighteenth century, did not stay all the year round in their estates in the country. London held many attractions and also duties, since four of the Molesworth baronets served as members of parliament for over forty-three years between 1701 and 1790. With no records to guide us, we can only assume, Westminster obligations apart, that the attractions which the capital held for the Molesworths were those of a social nature, similar to those which drew other aristocratic families to London at that time. It is known only that, after the fashion of the time of their social class, members of the Molesworth family were keen to have their likenesses captured on canvas. The appointments' book of Sir Joshua Reynolds records that members of the family sat for him on several occasions. In July 1755, John, later the 5th baronet, sat on four occasions and, in the same year, his brother, William, and his sister-in-law Anne also sat for the artist (these portraits hang in the dining-room at Pencarrow). John Molesworth, in the uniform of a colonel in the Cornish militia was painted in 1762, and again in 1766 after he had succeeded to the baronetcy (both these portraits are also to be found hanging in the dining-room). Finally, Sir William Molesworth sat for his portrait in March 1780. The family, when staying in London, after the fashion of the time, will have leased and not owned a 'town' house, but it is known that the 6th Baronet was having a house built in 'Mary bone Fields, Westminster' in the 1790s.

It is only at the very end of the eighteenth century that it is possible to gain some insight into developments in the gardens at Pencarrow. This information is gleaned from the letters of an ordinary locally-based working class family, one of whose members worked at Pencarrow for at least twenty-five years over the turn of the century, and two recent discoveries - a bundle of estate accounts in the Molesworth-St. Aubyn papers in the Cornwall County Record Office, and a manuscript record of some Pencarrow plant lists dating from c.1820. Dr Austin, the editor of *The Clift Family Correspondence, 1792-1846*, points out that the letters were written by the children of a journeyman miller and his wife, Robert (1725-84) and Joanna, née Courts (1733-87) Clift, who can have received, at best, only a rudimentary education and yet, their youngest son, William (1775-1849), as a result of his precocious artistic talents, bettered himself to the extent of achieving fame and fortune in London, culminating in his election as a Fellow of the Royal Society in 1823. It is to William Clift that we are indebted for the preservation of the family letters,[1] eighteen of which were written by John Clift (1759-1819), the eldest son. John Clift was born at the mill at Glyn in the parish of Cardinham, and was baptised in the parish church 30 September 1759. It is not known when he began to work at Pencarrow – he alludes in a letter of August 1793 to an apprenticeship served under his 'old master', Richard Tabb, the carpenter 'in residence' at Pencarrow until his death in November 1796 - but he was certainly lodging on the estate when the correspondence starts in February 1792. Clift was employed as carpenter/painter/handyman, and, in 1804, married Anne (Nancy) Menhennit, the dairymaid at the mansion, before being promoted to a supervisory role at Pencarrow in the last years of his life.

The records of the Pencarrow estate are the accounts submitted by the Pencarrow Steward of the time, John Symons to Messrs Efford & Foot, the 'Devisors of Sir William Molesworth Baronet, Deceased.' They itemise payments made to estate employees and local tradesmen for the years 1797-8, 1802, 1806-08 and 1809. What is of particular import are the payments made to George Bavin, the gardener, which were as follows:

	£	s	d	Notes
13 October 1797	105	0	0	
30 November 1797	25	0	0	
14 February 1798	70	0	0	
30 July 1798	140	19	6	in full to 31 May last
18 August 1798	82	0	6½	in full
3 February 1801	34	18	9	per bill
2 May 1802	50	11	0	bill for new plantation at the head of the park
1 January 1806	51	14	9	his salary, plants, labour etc.
17 January 1807	39	12	0	his bill, including 1 year's salary as Surveyor of woods
10 February 1808	51	7	6	

These payments obviously constitute an incomplete record of the amount Bavin may have spent on the garden/grounds of Pencarrow, and are not sufficiently itemised for it to be clear what proportion of the payments made to him were spent on plants for the garden, although they are specifically mentioned in Bavin's bill paid in January 1806. We do not know what the gardener's wages were, what his salary as Surveyor of the Woods amounted to, nor what proportion of his 'bills' was represented by labour costs – we do not even have the total payments recorded in a calendar year, nor do we have any other information about George Bavin except that he was sufficiently trusted by Sir William to be asked to sign and witness a legal document in December 1794. At most we know what was paid out by the Steward to George Bavin in a ten month period, October

1797 – August 1798. This amounted to £423.0s.0d., or an astonishing 49% of John Symons's total disbursements during that period and equivalent to thirty-five times John Clift's annual salary of £12.10s as an estate carpenter. Undoubtedly, some of the money will have gone, as it did in 1802, to restocking/replanting the woodland surrounding the park – since, then as now, the production of timber was looked upon as a long-term investment and Rudolph Ackermann, writing in 1826 described some 'fine plantations' at Pencarrow - but, at the turn of the century the fashion for the picturesque park, easy to create and not costly to maintain, with grass coming all the way up to the house was changing to allow formal, colourful beds of flowers, gravel paths and terraces near the house to break the plain expanse of green. It would have been expensive to create these new features, but there is no sign of any of them in the 1826 engraving of the south front of the house. Sir William, 6th baronet died in February 1798, leaving his son, Arscott, then aged seven, to succeed him.

We know from letters in The Clift Correspondence that Pencarrow was closed down after Sir William's death, only John Clift and two other men were kept on to look after the house and 'Ceep(sic) it in good repare (sic).' No fires were to be lit in the house for a year, and John Clift was apprehensive that it might become a ruin, since the plaster on the front of the house was already crumbling and falling off by the middle of 1799. In fact, although the Steward's accounts show that running repairs were carried out periodically, the house was still unfurnished in 1812, when Sir Arscott, by then married and with two children, announced his intention to come and reside at Pencarrow for the first time since his father's death fourteen years earlier.

It is true that a mention in one of John Clift's letters suggests that the Reverend John Molesworth periodically visited Pencarrow during these years, perhaps to keep an eye on the house and gardens. John Molesworth was the step-brother of the 6th baronet and so uncle to Sir Arscott and, from 1788 until his death in 1811, he was the Rector of the nearby church of St. Breock, a living in the gift of the Molesworth family. It would have been appropriate for the Reverend Molesworth to hold a watching, or even advisory brief on the garden at Pencarrow, for C.S.Gilbert in his *Historical Survey of the County of Cornwall* (1817), compliments him on the great improvements he had brought about in the garden of the St Breock 'parsonage house'.

Nevertheless, however George Bavin spent his money, it seems a great and disproportionate amount to spend on the garden/grounds of

Pencarrow over a number of years when none of the Molesworths were in residence.

The turn of the century saw a rise in the number of provincial nurseries and professional seedsmen. In the west country, William Lucombe's nursery at St Thomas's near Exeter had been long established (1720) and it later spawned a seedsman's shop in Exeter in the 1790s; the famous Veitch nursery (so well patronised by the 8th baronet in his reconstruction of the garden in the 1830s and 1840s) was founded also in Exeter in 1808, but there was a nurseryman/seedsman much closer to Pencarrow who had been trading from as early as the 1780s. William, John Clift's younger brother, was employed for about two years in the 1790s by George King, in Bodmin, where he learned about 'budding and grafting, putting down layers and transplanting seedling plants.' He wrote also of the 'cucumber frames and glass shades which protected the young cuttings of geraniums and myrtles', and that he became a 'tolerable botanist and horticulturist.'

The King nursery may not have cultivated the exotic plants which were becoming all the rage at the turn of the century, but they were certainly being cultivated in private gardens in Cornwall by that time. The mild, equable climate of the county was well suited to the cultivation of plant species indigenous to climates warmer than other parts of England; there was a ready means for Cornish landowners to obtain seeds from the voyages of the Falmouth packets, and there is evidence that, although the emergence of the greenhouse/hothouse as we know it is generally accepted to date from J.C. Loudon's patent of 1816, suitable structures had been used in Cornwall for some years before. For example, Charles Rashleigh (1747-1823) with money made from tin, copper and china clay, established Charlestown harbour and built Duporth House nearby, where he laid out and cultivated the gardens 'with much care. After his death in 1823, the *Cornwall Gazette* carried a notice advertising an auction of Rashleigh's 'valuable collection of Stove, Exotic and Green-House Plants.' Also the *Gardener's Magazine* of 1830 recorded the interest taken in hardy, exotic plants by Thomas Rutger, the head gardener of the Molesworth's relations, the St. Aubyn family, at their estates of St Michael's Mount and Clowance. Moreover, confirmation of the interest in and cultivation of greenhouse/hothouse plants at Pencarrow early in the nineteenth century has come to light in *A List of Green house and Hot House Plants at Pencarrow* recently discovered in the archives at Pencarrow.

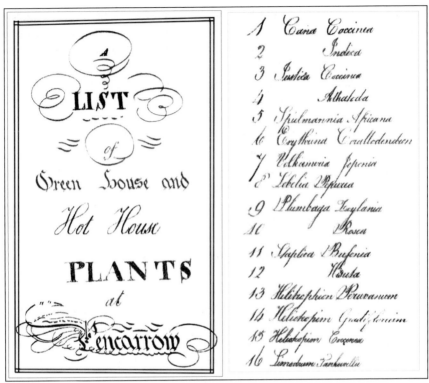

List of Hot-House Plants c.1822

The plants in the *List* are listed by categories in a thirty-page manuscript booklet. All but the entries for 1822 on the last two pages are undated, but must have been compiled prior to that year and, except for the 1822 entries, they were written by one hand. The List poses some interpretive problems: the Latin names are not always correctly spelled; some plants have been renamed since the start of the nineteenth century rendering the original names meaningless; plants which may have been considered 'frost tender' when they were first introduced to Cornwall have, over the years, become 'frost hardy', and would not nowadays even be wintered in a greenhouse and, included in the List are plants which, like the ericas and roses would not, even in the 1820s, have been housed in a greenhouse or hothouse. The first category of plants listed are not a generic group, but are a collection of flowers and flowering shrubs all of which would have needed protection from the frost in winter, or from the elements generally as seedlings prior to being planted out. There are 211 plants listed in the first category, and they are all flowers (e.g. canna, lobelia, hoya, tradiscantia, protea, verbena, gardenia, salvia, amaryllis, gladiolus, pelargonium, echium, geranium, mimulus, vinca), or flowering shrubs (e.g. plumbago, hibiscus, bignonia, passiflora, diosma, mimosa, acacia, jasmine, magnolia, pittosporum, leptospermum, hypericum), all of which would have needed the protection of a greenhouse or a hothouse.

The second category is of heaths and this contains 52 varieties of ericas or heathers which, nowadays, would be planted out all year round. It is possible in the 1820s that the plants were kept small and in pots in a greenhouse which served as an alpine house. The third category is a list of 133 Herbaceous and American Plants. Here again are flowers (phlox, helianthus, rudbeckia, saxifrage, achillea, viola, clematis, veronica, camp-anula, delphinium, peony) and flowering shrubs (azalea, rhododendron, daphne, spiraea), but they are, in the main, 'frost hardy' and would not require any artificial protection.

The third category lists 111 varieties of roses – again a plant more at home in an outdoor rose or cutting garden rather than a greenhouse unless, perhaps, they were being cultivated without risk of infection to provide material for pot-pourri. The final entries for 1822 are of five roses, a purple magnolia, a Chinese almond tree, a white rhododendron and a cassia tree. Sadly, there is no indication of where the plants, their seeds or bulbs were obtained, but the exotic plants in need of protection will have been housed in hothouses just identifiable in the 1813 Ordnance Survey map. They were located, together with what appears to be a walled garden to the east of the mansion where the garden borders the track to Trescowe. These, in turn, were replaced by a range of half a dozen stoves and hothouses erected by the 8th baronet in c.1840 which stood for the remainder of the nineteenth century, until they were dismantled c.1912. The brick rear wall of the 1840 buildings still stands and limits the border in the garden recently been adopted by the Friends of Pencarrow at the north end of the east lawn.

Pencarrow is described briefly in three books published in the 1820s. C.S. Gilbert, in 1820, wrote that the 'gardens and shrubberies are large and flourishing;' F.W.L. Stockdale, in 1824, wrote that the 'gardens and hot-houses are very beautiful, and kept in excellent order,' and Rudolf Ackermann, in 1826, described the gardens as 'very extensive and most advantageously planned, with hot-houses, which produce as fine fruit as any place in the county.' We know from an engraving by Stockdale published by Ackermann, that there were no flower beds on the south side of the house; the north side of the house looked on to a cobbled courtyard and domestic buildings, and the kitchens and housekeeper's quarters looked out to the west. Consequently, the gardens which were described can only have been sited to the east of the house as suggested by the 1813 O.S. map. A photograph of the glasshouses captures them as they were in 1902, little if any altered since their erection. They stand at the northern edge of the east lawn, bordered by flower beds, and shrubs can be seen planted in the lawn in front of the glasshouses. W.F.R writing in the *Gardeners' Chronicle* in 1842, describes a plot of ground in front of the glasshouses planted with an interesting collection of New Zealand plants and also a bed of 'gladioluses'*(sic)*. Until the creation of the Italian garden in the 1830s, it is possible that other flower beds were set into the east lawn since, in very dry weather, it is possible to discern outlines in the grass which would support this hypothesis.

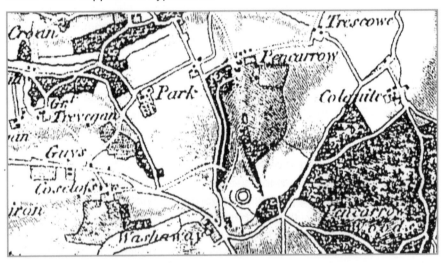

Ackermann was in no doubt about where the credit lay for the admirable state of the garden, writing 'much praise is due to Lady Molesworth for many of the improvements, particularly in the grounds; also for the cultivation of many choice plants and shrubs.' Lady Mary Molesworth (1779-1877), neé Brown was the wife of Sir Arscott Ourry Molesworth, the 6th baronet. She came from a Scottish family from Edinburgh and, if she was indeed the creator of the improvements in the gardens, it may well be that she got her inspiration in the first place from influences in her native city. After Oxford, Edinburgh had been the first city in Britain to establish a botanic garden as early as 1670, but it was in the second half of the eighteenth century that the Scottish capital achieved a pre-eminent position

134

as a centre of botanical learning very largely through teaching and activities of John Hope, Professor of Medicine and Botany at the University.

In 1764, a society of persons interested in planting, gardening and agriculture was formed in Edinburgh 'for the importation of foreign seeds from different parts of the globe, but chiefly from America.' By the end of the century an ever-increasing number of commercial gardens had sprung up in Britain, and seedsmen, nurserymen and florists were publishing plant and seed catalogues, seven of which are listed by John Harvey as having been produced by firms trading in Edinburgh in the last quarter of the eighteenth century. Clearly, for anyone growing up with the interest in gardening and matters horticultural attributed to her by Rudolph Ackermann, the Edinburgh-born Mary Brown, will have found herself in an exciting and stimulating horticultural environment.

Mary Brown married Sir Arscott Ourry Molesworth in Edinburgh in 1809, and they first came to reside in Pencarrow in 1812. But, if we conjecture that Mary Molesworth inspired the 'improvements' in the gardens at Pencarrow, who was it who put her plans into practice? From the estate accounts already referred to, we know that George Bavin was the gardener until at least 1811. Egloshayle parish records reveal that the gardener (head gardener?) from 1816-21 was Daniel Mackenzie. James Mackenzie, son of Daniel and Margaret was baptised 3 July, 1816 and further children were baptised 26 December, 1817 (christened Arscott!), 4 September, 1818 and 21 January, 1821. Two factors indicate that Mackenzie, not Bavin was responsible for the implementing improvements in the gardens: firstly, some of the varieties of plants listed in the glasshouses can have been named only after the Napoleonic wars. In particular, the following pelargoniums: no.141, Blucher (Marshal Blucher commanded the Prussian army at Waterloo), no.142, Regent (the future George IV was Prince Regent 1811-1820), no.143, Royal George, no. 144, Bentinck (Lord William Bentinck, an army general who fought under Wellington), no. 145, Wellington, no.146, Princess Charlotte (1796-1817), only daughter of the Prince Regent) and no. 153, Commander-in-Chief. It is not clear when Mackenzie ceased to be the gardener at Pencarrow, or when William Crawford (who died 'in post' in 1838) took his place but, after the death of her husband (December 1823), and Catherine, one of her daughters, (February 1824), Mary Molesworth returned to Edinburgh with her remaining children and did not return to Pencarrow until her son, William, the 8th baronet, came of age in 1831.

Mary Molesworth was obviously attached to her native country and naturally, by extension, to her countrymen. When her son William set out on his 'grand tour' in 1829, it was a family friend from Edinburgh, General Sir Joseph Straton, whom she asked to act as his guardian abroad, and she engaged another Scotsman, Duncan Maclean, to serve as his manservant. Maclean served his master loyally until Sir William died in 1855, and he ended his days living in retirement at Pencarrow, having married Rebecca (née Ford) who became the housekeeper of the mansion (c.1850). Maclean, Mackenzie and Crawford are not Cornish, nor even English surnames. They are unambiguously Scottish, and it is surely not inconceivable that Mary Molesworth brought the last two named from Scotland to carry out her plans for the garden at the ancestral seat of her husband's family, particularly since, as Toby Musgrave, the author of *The Head Gardeners*, has stated, Scotland at that time was regarded as 'fertile ground' for the training of gardeners.

There can be no doubt that Sir William Molesworth, rightly deserves his high reputation as the architect of the gardens of Pencarrow as we know them today, but the argument put forward in this paper surely indicates that his mother, Mary, and her Scottish gardeners, deserve greater recognition than they have ever received for their earlier 'improvements' to the garden.

P.S. An intriguing coincidence emerged in the course of the research for this paper. In 1808/9 Sir Thomas Acland (who was in the process of landscaping and planting his estate at Killerton near Exeter) and his wife 'wintered' in Edinburgh. Sir Arscott Molesworth and Mary Brown were married in Edinburgh in July, 1809. The Killerton estate was laid out by John Veitch (1752-1839), a Scot, who later founded the eponymous nursery near Exeter, and Mary Molesworth was, about to make changes to the garden at Pencarrow with the help of another Scot, Daniel Mackenzie. Could the parties concerned have met and conferred? After all, their estates were in the west country, Acland and Molesworth were both baronets; they would have moved in the same stratum of society, and the gardening scene in Scotland at that time was such that Veitch and Mackenzie may well have been acquainted or known of each other!

Reference

1. The relevant Clift letters are to be found in the British Library Add. Mss 39955. I am grateful to Dr Austin for allowing me to quote from her work.

'A *Really Good* Gardener', Thomas Corbett
Head Gardener (1837 - 1848)

In the autumn of 1836, Sir William Molesworth learned that William Crawford, his head gardener, whom he held in high regard, and had charged with implementing his plans for the new layout and planting of his gardens at Pencarrow, was 'dying of a consumption.' He began to look for a replacement to carry on his grand design but, as he pointed out in a letter to a friend, he was seeking to appoint a gardener out of the ordinary. 'I am in want of a *good* one', he wrote,' but he must be a *really good* one, able not only to look after gardens, but understand plantations.' In fact, Crawford did not die until early November 1838 but, by then, Sir William had appointed a worthy successor in Thomas Corbett. Corbett served as head gardener until his death in 1848, by which time Sir William's garden designs had been laid out, and the bulk of the new planting of shrubs and trees had taken place.

Head Gardeners

In the eighteenth century, the prestige of British landowners stemmed principally from the architectural ostentation of their family seats and the vistas created by landscaping the surrounding parkland. By the 1830s, however, the botanical content and the pictorial appeal of the gardens immediately adjacent to a stately home acquired greater importance. The Capability Browns and Humphry Reptons of the eighteenth century had primarily been skilled surveyors and landscape gardeners of perspective vision. In the nineteenth century, head gardeners were additionally expected to be proficient botanists, plant physiologists and imaginative plantsmen. They could be faced with the challenge of various types of garden – from the humdrum kitchen garden to the formal, exotic, tropical, rockery, fernery, water garden, herb garden, orchards and the management of greenhouses, hot-houses and ice-houses. Moreover, a head gardener had to be dependable and trustworthy since, although technically a mere employee, he enjoyed a great degree of independence and was in control of a sizeable annual budget. More than ever before, there existed a greater degree of trust, familiarity, even friendship, between landowner and head gardener – the example of the close relationship at Chatsworth between the 6th Duke of Devonshire and Joseph Paxton is perhaps the most memorable.

On his return in 1831 from his 'grand tour', fired with enthusiasm (particularly by what he had seen in the gardens of Italy), Sir William Molesworth was intent on redesigning and developing the gardens of Pencarrow. William Crawford started to execute the new designs by creating an Italian garden in place of the lawn to the South of the mansion. When it became evident that Crawford's mortal illness would not allow him to carry out all that he had in mind for the gardens of Pencarrow, Sir William set about finding a new head gardener. He was seeking to appoint someone with the knowledge, experience and aptitude to realise his plans, but also someone determined to keep abreast of horticultural developments, keen to master new techniques and someone who was not afraid to experiment and be innovative. He found such a man in Thomas Corbett.

Early History

Thomas, the eldest son of the marriage of William Corbett and Elizabeth Maughan, was born at Sandhoe, near Hexham in Northumberland, in the parish of St. John Lee and was baptised on 27 May, 1798.

Sir John Lee Church

Nothing is known of the Corbett family circumstances, or of Thomas's childhood years, but it is clear from his eventual career, and what little writing in his own hand that has survived (see Appendix A), that he received a sound educational grounding in the 'three Rs'. Although the area surrounding Sandhoe had many coal and lead mines, the soil was rich and the land was a principal source of employment when Thomas was growing up. It was also an age in which country mansions were developing their grounds and gardens, and if Thomas set out to be a gardener in his youth, there was one stately home in the parish, Beaufront Castle, for long the seat of the Errington family, where he might have served a gardening apprenticeship – all the more likely since census records (1841 and 1851) reveal that Thomas's younger brother, Edward, was employed as a male servant and later as a footman at Beaufront Castle. In 1810, by which time Corbett would have started a gardening apprenticeship, Beaufront Castle was described as 'Few places make a finer appearance, or enjoy a larger or better cultivated prospect than this.' At the turn of the eighteenth/nineteenth

Beaufront Castle

centuries, John Errington spent £20,000 on the gardens, plantations, lawns, hot-houses - an ideal situation for a budding head gardener.

Thomas Corbett next surfaced in Kirkdale, North Yorkshire, where he married Elizabeth Pickering in St.Gregory's Minster, the parish church, on 22 August 1822.

By the time the couple's first child was born the following year, the family had moved to Kilnwick Percy, South Yorkshire, where their son, William, was baptised in St. Helen's church on 2 November, 1823. They were still living in the same parish when their next child, Ann Elizabeth, was baptised on 12 June 1825 but, although it is known from the 1841 census return that a further daughter

St. Gregory's Minster, Kirkdale

was born two years later, the family had moved away from Kilnwick Percy by the summer of 1827. In the early 1820s, the inhabitants of Kilnwick Percy numbered only 43 and, almost certainly, they would all have been dependant for employment on the house and estate of the Dennison family at Kilnwick Percy Hall. The Hall was a handsome Georgian stone mansion, fronted by a spacious lawn and lake and surrounded by extensive pleasure grounds.

The Missing Years

How and why Thomas moved his family to Kilnwick Percy is uncertain, but it has to be assumed that he made the move to further his gardening career on Robert Dennison's estate. Even more unaccountable

© Colin Hinson (colin@blunham.demon.co.uk)

Kilnwick Percy Hall

are his movements in the next ten years or so. A family descendant is of the opinion that he may have been the Thomas Corbett, seedsman and florist, of West Ham, Essex, who was bankrupted in July 1835 with debts of £100, but there is uncertainty about his whereabouts and his activities until he was engaged by Sir William, although it is known that he was the foreman of one of the two Pontey's nurseries in Plymouth immediately prior to his appointment as head gardener at Pencarrow in 1837.

We do know, however, that in 1827 Thomas Corbett became a father for the third time on the birth of a second daughter, Mary Esther, who was born on 27 July and subsequently baptised in the parish church of St. Mary,

Rotherhithe, Surrey on 31 August 1827. Thomas's profession was recorded as a 'superintendent'. There was no indication of what he superintended, but in the Commercial Dock at Rotherhithe there were warehouses deigned to store grain and seeds, so it may be that one of these was in his charge. Corbett's address in the baptismal record was given as 'Surrey Canal'[2], expanded three years later to 'The Grand Surrey Dock' in his application for election as a Fellow of the Linnean Society of London in February 1830. (see Appendix C). The Society, the first specialist scientific society outside the Royal Society, was and is still the world's leading society for the study and promotion of all aspects of natural history, including botany. There are three categories of individual membership: Student, Associate and Fellow. Candidates for membership must be supported by at least two Fellows and are subject to election. Fellows are entitled to use the designation FLS after their names.

Fellow of the Linnean Society

Neither the parish records of 1827 recording the birth of Esther Mary Corbett, nor the November 1829 letter of recommendation to the Linnean Society provides a precise address for Corbett, but his application was supported by a letter signed by some eminent contemporary names in the fields of natural history and horticulture who recommended him as 'A Gentleman much attached to the study of Natural History': Thomas Bell FRS, FLS (1792-1880) was a zoologist and future President of the Linnean Society; John Claudius Loudon FLS (1783-1843) was a botanist, a prolific horticultural writer, garden designer and garden magazine editor; George Sinclair FLS (1787-1834) was head gardener to the Duke of Bedford at his Woburn estate 1807-25, and later went into partnership as a seedsman with John Cormack (father and son) in New Cross in Surrey. Sinclair was renowned as **the** authority of his day on the cultivation of grasses, and it is generally recognised that the results of his experiments at Woburn subsequently influenced Darwin's theory of evolution by natural selection. Corbett's remaining two supporters were less distinguished: George Charlwood FLS (1784-1861) was a seedsman in Covent Garden, and James Thomas Carey, about whom the only fact known is that he was not a Fellow of the Linnean Society.

The letter makes it clear that all the signatories knew Corbett personally and considered him a worthy candidate but, frustratingly, they do not indicate the particular sphere of Corbett's 'attachment' to natural history, nor do they give any indication of why they were confident that he would prove a 'valuable and useful member.' Of his supporters, we know Corbett had great respect for Loudon, and that he regarded Sinclair as a friend. It is not clear how he came to know them but, although no proof has been found, it is not without the bounds of possibility that, during the missing years, Corbett may have been a business associate or acquaintance of Sinclair and/or Charlwood. In any event, by the time he took up his appointment at Pencarrow, he was sufficiently '*au fait*' with nurseries in London to know which to recommend so that Sir William might admire the 'most beautiful collection of camellias' (2,000 blooms), a sight which surpassed the baronet's wildest imagination.

Thomas Corbett's letter of recommendation to the Linnean Society [3]

Why and when Corbett made the move from the Grand Surrey Docks to Pontey's nursery in Plymouth remains a mystery, but we know that

Sir William bought plants from the nursery, and it is there that their paths will have crossed. There were, in fact, two Pontey nurseries in Plymouth in the 1830s, and both were described in *The Gardeners' Magazine* in 1842 by J.C. Loudon. Mr John Pontey, junior, had a nursery in Cornwall Street. in the heart of the city, but this was devoted to fruit trees and a pear orchard in particular, while his father, by then an octogenarian, had the larger nursery at Vinstone (two miles to the north west of the city centre) where Thomas Corbett was employed as the foreman., and which featured an arboretum of an extensive collection of trees and shrubs. Here the houses and stoves contained a large collection of exotic plants imported from South America and the Cape (South Africa), and they were all heated by 'Corbett's open gutters, which Mr Pontey and all other nurserymen who have tried it, agree in most strongly recommending.'

Corbett's 'Mode of Heating by Hot Water'

Thomas Corbett's patent application for 'Certain Improvements in heating hot-houses and other buildings', was submitted in August, 1838, and was, quite simply, a system for heating hot-houses by circulating hot water in open gutters, described rather grandiloquently as his 'hygro-thermanic apparatus' in *The Gardeners' Magazine*. It does not appear to have been supported by any drawings, nor does it appear ever to have been subsequently registered as a patent. Descriptions of his 'mode of heating' were, however, published in the *Gardeners' Magazine* in January and February, 1841, of the system as used, not only in Pontey's nursery, but also in another nursery in Exeter (Lucombe and Pine) and in the garden of a Mrs Wells in Cowley near Exeter. The dimensions and construction materials used differed, but the fundamental principles were the same. A large boiler was installed to heat water, which was then passed from the top of the boiler through an iron pipe along an open trough (formed of cast iron or slabs of slate jointed together, 6" wide at the top, 4" wide at the bottom and 7" deep), running the length of the hot-house to the end from where it was returned to the bottom of the boiler by way of a 4" iron pipe. The open trough produced a humid heat but, by means of fitting covers or lids, this could be regulated to produce a 'perfect command of heat with an atmosphere in every respect congenial to vegetation.' A Mr Glendinning writing to the Gardener's Chronicle in 1841 strongly recommended Corbett's system, writing that 'Mr. Corbett, by his invention, has done much to advance horticulture and conferred a great boon on fellow gardeners. 'Sadly, as we shall see, the originality of Corbett's system was challenged, and the invention did not make his fortune

The interest in Corbett's system and the publicity surrounding it, in particular Corbett's own advertisement and insistence on his patent rights being observed (see Appendix C), produced an immediate, scathing response in a letter published in *The Gardener's Chronicle* in February 1841. The author, signing himself simply 'S', disputed Corbett's claim of originality, citing several earlier examples of heating by the same principles, and he questioned the validity of the patent maintaining that Corbett had failed to produce the necessary specifications for his system within the six month time limit after registering his application. 'S' concluded with the patronisingly caustic comment 'This case ought to teach persons in his [Corbett's] station of life not to depend too much on the fancied originality of their own inventions, but to consult with those best informed on the subject they are engaged upon.' With the support of Loudon, the editor of *The Gardener's Magazine*, it appears that Corbett may have defended his position for some time but, shortly after Loudon's death in 1843, Corbett wrote to his son, William, that his 'hot water licences are quite stopped; Rendle[4] has advertised everywhere that it is his invention and no-one has a right to pay me ....it is now called Rendle's tank system and I have never moved to contradict it as I have no money to go to Law.' At least Corbett had the satisfaction of knowing that his system, installed in the hot-houses after his arrival at Pencarrow, came fully up to the expectations of his employer. Moreover, in an account of Pencarrow published in The Gardener's Chronicle in August 1842, the reviewer found that 'the hygro-thermatic apparatus answers well as the plants appear to grow in great luxuriance.' Was it a coincidence that the article appeared above the initials WER, or was it intentionally a cruelly ironic action of pouring salt into a wound inflicted by **W**illiam **E**dgcumbe **R**endle?

By the time Corbett became head gardener; Sir William Molesworth and William Crawford had started to implement Sir William's plans for the redevelopment of the gardens of Pencarrow. The lawn in front of the house had been converted into a terraced, Italianate garden with decorative urns and a fountain in the middle, and it contained flower beds with a rich and colourful variety of bedding plants; elsewhere in the grounds some shrubs (rhododendrons and azaleas) had been introduced, together with the beginnings of Sir William's rare conifer collection (including the *Araucaria imbricata* which was to be given its common name of 'monkey puzzle tree' by a visitor to Pencarrow), but it was Thomas Corbett who, before his death in 1848, largely implemented the designs which Sir William had in mind –

structural, as in the rockery, plant houses, lake, and the ice house, and horticultural in the challenge of cultivating the great variety of trees and plants, native and exotic, which the baronet was keen to introduce into the gardens, in addition Corbett fully discharged his responsibilities in the kitchen garden.

The Rockery

It is generally accepted that the boulders which form the basis of the impressive rockery at Pencarrow were brought there free of charge from Bodmin Moor by Sir William Molesworth's tenant farmers and local tradesmen, to show their affection and loyalty for a beneficent landlord, a generous patron and a popular MP. In his early years in parliament (1832-6), the baronet's ill-concealed opposition to the prejudices and privileges of the land-owning aristocracy and squirearchy endeared him to the yeomanry and bourgeoisie of his constituency of East Cornwall. The boulders were brought to Pencarrow just as Thomas Corbett succeeded William Crawford.

Sir William's sister, Mrs Mary Ford, writing in 1900, remembered that the rockery had taken some three years to construct, and Alison Adburgham in her biography of the 8th Molesworth baronet entitled *A Radical Aristocrat*, wrote that between forty and fifty carts were used to transport the boulders, and that Sir William, himself, supervised the placing of every single block of granite. This last assertion is an unjustified exaggeration. Sir William, while he was a member of parliament, was inevitably London-based and, in the light of his other literary and political commitments in the capital, his visits to Pencarrow in the mid-1830s were infrequent and not of long duration. The recent discovery of a letter from Sir William to his sister Mary reveals that the baronet was quite prepared to give credit where it was due in the construction of the rockery. Sir William wrote from Pencarrow in the summer of 1837 to his sister in London, 'Pencarrow is looking excessively well. I am delighted with the rock-work, which Corbett has executed with skill and ability. It accurately resembles nature, so that a stranger would easily fancy it real.' It is true that, after Sir William had retired from Parliament for the second time in June 1841, he spent much of the next three years at Pencarrow where he supervised a very active period of design and planting in the garden but, by then, all the boulders had been delivered and the rockery had been established and planted by Thomas Corbett.

Two contemporary pictures of the South front of Pencarrow are informative. An unsigned pen and watercolour-wash illustration dating from the early 1830s, shows the Italian garden already laid out, terraced and planted, but there are no boulders in evidence on the bank on the East side.

The Italian Garden c. 1832/4

A lithograph by C.J. Greenwood engraved for printing in E.Twycross's *Mansions of England & Wales*, published in 1846, shows the rockery in its infancy. The boulders to the South of the Italian garden appear to be the first to have been arranged since the vegetation here is already established, whereas the area to the East of the garden reveals the bare rocks apparently haphazardly placed.

The Italian Garden & Rockery, 1846

By August 1842, Pencarrow was already recognised as 'one of the first places in the West of England' and the 'large and extensive mass of rockwork, very naturally arranged' was one of the principal attractions according to W.E.R. writing in *The Gardeners' Chronicle*. He acknowledged the major role played by Sir William Molesworth ('a spirited proprietor') in the making of the garden, but he credits Thomas Corbett with the creation and siting of the rockery. According to the account, before the rockery was constructed, there had been a hillock on the East side of the newly-created Italian garden, and the rockery was deliberately designed to disguise the unsightly appearance of the hillock from the house. W.E.R. was particularly impressed by the fact that the boulders – some as heavy as two or three tons - had not been dug out of a quarry, but had been lifted from the surface of Bodmin moor with lichen and moss growing on them, giving them a most natural look. He was also intrigued by the artificial bog which had been created in the middle of the rockery fed by constantly running water, and by the number and variety of plants already established. He mentioned particularly, different species of *Mahonia*; a *Dionaea muscipula* (Venus's fly-trap) which had survived a bitter winter with only a bell jar for protection; *Pinguicula grandiflora* and *Parnassia Caroliniana*. Among the trees planted and already established were 'a fine and glorious specimen of *Araucaria imbricata* about 5½ ft. in height, and a 'vigorous plant of the *Cedrus deodara*.' The rockery was, in the opinion of W.E.R., 'a great ornament.'

The Hot-Houses

When F.W.L.Stockdale visited Pencarrow in 1824, shortly after the death of Sir Arscott Ourry Molesworth, the 7th baronet, he remarked that the 'hot-houses are kept in excellent order', and Rudolph Ackermann writing two years later maintained that the hot-houses produced 'as fine fruit as any place in the county', and there is in existence a list (c.1822) of the plants they contained. It is possible that these houses were sited in the area of the walled fruit garden (to the north of the present car park), since they are not in evidence in the early 1830s, but a range of glass-houses is clearly visible in the 1846 lithograph, and there are indications in some tantalisingly isolated references in the Pencarrow archive, that these were constructed c.1840 (Sir William's accounts show that he paid a Mr Harper £156.13s.10d for building a greenhouse in that year) and were completed in 1843.

There is no mention of hot-houses after 1910, and it must be presumed that the decision by Sir Lewis Molesworth, 10th baronet, (who inherited Pencarrow on the death of Mary Ford in March of that year) not to reside at Pencarrow, and the subsequent cost-cutting exercise which Sir Lewis carried out in respect of the Pencarrow mansion and garden when, like the Italian garden, the hot-houses will have been deemed a costly extravagance. The departure of the then head gardener, Aubrey

Bartlett, shortly afterwards contributed either to their immediate demolition by Sir Lewis, or to a neglect to the extent that they fell into disrepair and had to be demolished during, or shortly after the end of the 1914-18 war. They had certainly disappeared by the time Sir Hugh Molesworth-St. Aubyn and his family came to live at Pencarrow c.1920. All that remains now of the range of glass-houses in the garden is their rear South-facing wall which runs along the back of what has been adopted as the Friends of Pencarrow's flower border, and which, in season, is gloriously covered with *Wisteria sinensis* and *floribunda*. On the North side of this wall, there is a range of 20th century plant houses on either side of the structure with a slated roof which must have housed the boiler for Corbett's 1840s hygrothermanic heating system. There are indications in the brick work in the wall of the dimensions of some of the houses pictured but, sadly, there are no visible clues as to their individual purpose.

The Hot-Houses in 1902, sited on the North side of the East lawn (pictured shortly before they were pulled down)

Hot-houses built in a variety of materials had begun to appear in the gardens of the country mansions of the English aristocracy in the early 1700s, but with increasing numbers and species of exotic plants reaching this country from the expanding Empire and beyond in the 18th century, England's cold winter climate dictated a need to develop a dependably sympathetic ambience in which to cultivate them successfully. Glasshouses were considered to be the answer, but arguments raged about their design, and how best to glaze and heat them. Design was always largely a matter of taste, but glazing improved with the invention of glazing bars and the ridge and furrow roof in the 1820s, sheet glass in the 1830s and the removal of duty on glass in the 1840s. For many years, however, the favoured method of heating was by direct heating from coal fires and flues which ran from the furnace along the front and back of the houses. This method proved costly and inefficient and was supplanted, for a while, at the end of the 18th century by steam heat, but the boilers proved expensive, temperamental and with a tendency to explode. Eventually, shortly before Sir William ordered the construction of his new glass-houses, a system was developed whereby water heated by a boiler was circulated through the houses by means of enclosed cast-iron pipes, but it was difficult to control the temperature. Thomas Corbett's variation was to convert the pipes into troughs with detachable fitted covers and, by this system, and by the use of trays of water strategically placed to give off added moisture where needed, he was able to exert more effective control over the heat and humidity required in each of the houses in which the system was in use.

Stockdale and Ackermann who described Pencarrow in 1824 and 1826 respectively confirmed the existence of hot-houses, but they did not specify how many there were, where they were sited, nor what they housed. Ackermann mentioned the 'fine fruit' produced in them, and we learn from a letter written by Sir William in 1844 that he had had a 'splendid show of peaches and figs' that year, and that he had 'stuffed himself' with the latter. We also know where the houses were sited in Corbett's time, and we have some idea of the variety and purpose of each. W.E.R. described a greenhouse and a stove on his visit in 1842 and, in 1843, Sir William recorded in his *Planting Book* the construction of new hot-houses - 'a new vinery, an orchid-house and a camellia-house.' Elsewhere in his correspondence, Sir William mentioned a heath-house (1843) and a fern-house (1844).

The contents of the Pencarrow hot-houses in the course of the 19th century are revealing, but not without conundrums. The Latin, scientific names are not always correctly spelled, some have been renamed in the course of the century to render the first recorded meaningless, and plants considered 'frost tender' in the 1820s had become 'frost hardy' by the end of the century. The first category of plants recorded in the *List* of the early 1820s, consisted of a collection of flowers (*canna, lobelia, hoya, tradiscantia, protea, verbena, gardenia, salvia, amaryllis, gladiolus, pelargonium, echium, geranium, mimulus, vinca*), or flowering shrubs (*plumbago, hibiscus, bigonia, passiflora, diosma, mimosa, acacia, jasmine, magnolia, pittosporum, leptospermum, hypericum*), all of which would have been considered 'frost tender'. The second category contained 52 varieties

of *Ericas* or heathers which would, today, be considered 'frost hardy'. The third category, Herbaceous and American Plants, consisted of flowers – *phlox, helianthus, rudbeckia, saxifrage, achillea, viola, clematis, veronica, campanula, delphinium, peony* – and flowering shrubs – *azalea, rhododendron, daphne and spiraea* – the majority of which are now considered 'frost hardy'. The final category is quite the most puzzling, since it contained 111 varieties of roses, a plant more at home outdoors than in a hot-house. If, as Ackermann suggested in 1826, Lady Mary Molesworth, the wife and, after 1823, the widow of the 7th baronet, is to be credited with the 'cultivation of many choice plants and shrubs', it would appear that her selection of plants was based, to a great extent, on the colour and perfume each would produce. Is it possible that Lady Mary was an early pioneer of the 'bedding system' (growing plants in the hot-houses in the winter months to plant out in the garden in the summer) which was to become such a characteristic of the Victorian garden?

By 1842, the flowers and roses had totally disappeared from the hot-houses and, although colour remained an important consideration in the plants, so, too, had perfume. The stove housed a variety of *Orchidaceous* and other tropical plants, the greenhouse still contained a number of *Ericas*, and the *Fuchsia*-house contained a numerous collection including 'all the newest sorts, loaded with their beautiful, bright blossoms.' At this time Corbett was also experimenting with the plants sent to Pencarrow by Sir William's brother, Francis, from New Zealand, and he prepared a plot of ground in front of the greenhouse to test whether the plants would 'stand over the winter', and become, as hoped, 'a great benefit to the shrubberies and plantations' of the Pencarrow garden.

By 1878, when Edward Luckhurst visited Pencarrow, he found the range of glasshouses contained a large stove, a stove aquarium, a greenhouse, a *Fuchsia*-house, a fern-house and two small vineries. The stove and stove aquarium were again recorded in 1900, as were the two vineries but, by that time, a cool conservatory had been added together with a tropical rockery behind the stove. There is no record of the construction of any hot-houses/greenhouses at Pencarrow after 1843, so it is probable that the houses pictured were essentially what was built in Corbett's time, even though their plant content and purpose may have varied – for instance it would appear that plant foliage was the prime consideration in a hot-house plant for Corbett in the 1840s, and for his successors later in the century, just as the flower and the perfume of the plant had been compelling in the 1820s.

Having decided not to stand again for his constituency of Leeds in the General Election of 1841, Sir William Molesworth spent most of the next three years at Pencarrow. A lot of his time was devoted to a self-imposed literary project of collecting, editing and publishing the works of Thomas Hobbes of Malmesbury, a task which he had begun some years earlier, but he was also keen to develop his plans for the gardens at Pencarrow. With the Italian garden and the rockery laid out and the plant-houses completed, in 1842 Sir William supervised the re-routing of the carriage drive leading off the Bodmin-Launceston road to the mansion and the planting of rhodo-dendrons, hydrangeas and camellias backed by conifers on either side of the drive. He then turned his attention to the area to the south of the mansion, beyond the Italian garden, and Corbett was charged with carrying out his employer's designs for the valley leading up to and beyond the lake, the area now known as the American gardens.

The Lake

Until recently, it had been thought that the lake was created by Sir William Molesworth as part of his design for the valley, but further examination of the first Ordnance Survey map of Cornwall published in 1813, clearly shows, despite its frustratingly small scale, at least one lake/pond was already in existence at that date. Moreover, in the 1840 survey which followed the Commutation of Tithes Act of 1836, the two stretches of water were mapped as they are today, and the area described as 'Ponds and Plantation' covered twelve acres. Before the planting took place in the lower part of the valley, it might well have been possible to see the water in the distance from the house, but it is strange that Mary Ford in her recollections of the gardens before her brother's alterations and improvements, made no reference to any water feature, nor was it mentioned in the first detailed account of Sir William's innovations and future landscape plans which appeared above the initials WFR in the Gardeners' Chronicle in August 1842. What is indisputable, is that Sir William intended the higher stretch of water (which he more often than not called the pond) which is the lake as it is known today, to be a feature midway between the two halves of his American garden. Corbett planted the lake in 1843 with a variety of aquatic plants from 'the Cape' (South Africa), America together with some plants native to Britain. At the same time, the lower half of the American garden was planted with various species of gunnera, irises, pampas grass, sedges, bulrushes, bamboo and New Zealand flax, together with choice New Zealand and Tasmanian conifers, eucalyptus, elm and holm oak trees. In 1848, one of the last contributions made by Thomas Corbett before his death was to plant what Edward Luckhurst writing thirty years later described as 'the crowning glory of the valley', a rhododendron garden some two acres in extent beyond the lake. Corbett widened the paths, gravelled them and placed a granite seat at the head of the valley at the end of the path which Sir William dubbed 'the Lovers' Walk.'

The Ice-House

Like hot-houses, ice-houses had first been constructed in the estates of English country houses in the early 18th century when they were regarded as a luxury, but, by the middle of the following century, they had become a regular feature until their function was replaced by the chemical, mechanical and electrical advances which produced the refrigerators of the 20th century. Today, although the existence of as many as 3,000 ice-houses were recorded in a survey in the 1980s, most are now either derelict, destroyed or converted for reuse for other purposes, but the ice-house at Pencarrow, unused for more than a century, is more or less intact and its structure clearly discernible. Thomas Corbett, as a good head gardener, would have been fully conversant with the designs of ice-houses and all their requirements, and it would have been his responsibility to construct, maintain and manage the ice-house.

There was a lively debate in the columns of gardening magazines in the early 1840s about every aspect of ice-houses – location, access, construction, drainage, insulation, ventilation, ice-collection and methods of filling – Corbett participated in the debate, and he adopted what he considered to be best practice in the construction of the ice-house at Pencarrow. The precise date of construction is not known, but it is recorded in the tithe map of 1840, when it occupied an area of two perches (approx. eleven square yards). It was sited at the north-west corner of the lake (looking towards the mansion), and was built as an egg-shaped brick structure, with its entrance facing north, typifying the most successful and widely constructed underground storage chamber of that period, located as described by the architect John Papworth in 1819 in his *Rural Residences* 'in a retired spot in the grounds, and not far removed from water, and yet sufficiently elevated to be secure from damp,' and as illustrated in John Claudius Loudon's *Encyclopaedia of Cottage, Farm and Villa Architecture* (1833). It was situated in a rising bank close to the lake – a source of ice and an outlet for drainage – but it was not readily accessible from the mansion, even though a path to the emergent American gardens had been opened. It was not designed as an ornamental feature of the gardens, as was the case in many country houses, rather was it deliberately hidden and purely utilitarian exemplifying Corbett's input to the ice-house debate (see Appendix E) cited by Charles MacIntosh in his *The Book of the Garden (1853)*.

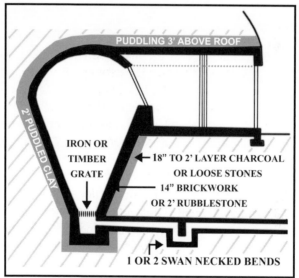

Section through a Single-Walled Ice-House
(Loudon's *Encyclopedia of Gardening*, 1828)

However, if the location of the ice-house at Pencarrow in the proximity of the lake is understandable, the fact that it is sited at a distance from the mansion, the kitchen gardens, greenhouses/hot-houses suggests that its principal function was not to serve as a ready larder for meat, game, or a cold store for the preservation of fruit and vegetables nor, despite Sir William's keen horticultural interests, is it likely that the ice-house was used extensively, as it was elsewhere, to retard or prolong the growth of ornamental plants. The ice-house was, simply, a building in which to store ice – ice to be used in the mansion in cold collations, cool drinks and exotic desserts when the family was in residence. Sadly, the archive at Pencarrow does not provide any information about the use to which the ice-house or its contents was put but there are two matter-of-fact entries for December, 1844 (co-incidentally the coldest month of the century to date). The first, for Saturday, 7th reads: 'Began to fill ice-house', and the second for Tuesday, 10th, 'Completed filling of the ice.'

The Ice-House by the lake at Pencarrow

The construction of the rockery and the ice-house may well be regarded as Thomas Corbett's lasting contributions to Sir William Molesworth's grand design for the garden at Pencarrow, but it is as a highly competent, innovative plantsman, rather than as a head gardener that he, himself, would wish to be remembered. He took in his stride his responsibility to keep the mansion supplied with cut flowers from the flower garden and produce from the kitchen garden and orchards, but he relished the challenge of siting, planting and nurturing exotic plants, shrubs and trees not native to this country, especially the conifers and the 'orchideous plants' which so captivated his employer, and he would not have wished for a greater tribute than that paid to him by Sir William in a letter written to his sister Mary in July 1844: 'I have not to deplore the loss or even the failure of a single plant.' High praise indeed!

Thomas Corbett suffered an apoplectic fit and died on 20 August, 1848. He was buried in the churchyard of his parish church in Egloshayle; his grave next to the grave of his first wife and close by the grave of William

Crawford, his predecessor at Pencarrow who had died ten years earlier. The 1841 census return records him living at Pencarrow with his wife, son and two daughters. We know, from parish records that his wife died of consumption on 12 October 1842, and from other sources we know that his son, William, sailed for New Zealand the following month, arriving in Port Nicholson, Wellington, North Island, in April 1843. William Corbett maintained the connection with the Molesworth family in so far as he was, for a year or so, employed by Francis Molesworth, Sir William's younger brother, who had himself in 1839 'departed [to New Zealand] on the arduous task of waging war with the wilderness and making it productive',[5] but who returned home suffering from ill health in April 1844 and died before he could go back to tame the wilderness in New Zealand. Much of the rest of our knowledge of Thomas `Corbett, can be gleaned from the only two letters written by him which have survived.

The first letter (first page copied in Appendix A and fully transcribed in Appendix B) was written in December, 1841 on behalf of the Wadebridge Farmers' Club, seeking assistance from Sir William Hooker, the first Director of the Royal Botanic Gardens at Kew. It reveals that Thomas Corbett was very much what was described in his day a 'scientific' gardener. Evidence of his thoughtful, intelligent and reasoned approach to horticultural challenges has already been illustrated in his hot water system for heating hot-houses, and in his contribution to the ice-house debate, but in this letter he reveals that his intellectual curiosity extended to a sphere of activity outside his strictly horticultural interests. The George Sinclair to whom Corbett refers, had been the superintendent gardener at Woburn Abbey. There, on instructions from the 6th Duke of Bedford, and under the supervision of Sir Humphry Davy, Sinclair designed a grass garden which was divided into 242 plots, each two feet square enclosed by wooden boards, in which he experimented and analysed the performance of different species of native grasses and herbs growing in different types of soil, with the aim of establishing and perfecting the best combination of forage grasses. Sinclair detailed the results of his experiments in *Hortus Gramineus Woburnensis* first published in 1816, and his conclusions, published in a 3rd edition in 1826, that a greater diversity of grasses planted in the experimental plots was responsible for greater production of plant matter - in other words the examination of the relationship between biodiversity and the functioning of ecosystems - not only influenced Darwin when he wrote his *Origin of Species* in 1859, but remains one of the burning issues in ecology to this day. The grass specimens which Corbett requested from Hooker were all of the *Gramineae* family and of the genus *Poa* (from the Greek for fodder), either rough meadow grass (*trivialis*) or smooth meadow grass (*pratensis*), and the Wadebridge farmers were clearly seeking to discover a mixture which would produce the best nutritional value. Sadly, as the records of the Farmers' Club have not survived, the outcome of Corbett's request is unknown, but we do know from W.F. Karkeek's *Report on the Farming of Cornwall* written in 1846, that Corbett was credited with 'having paid more attention to the growing of grasses than any other person in Cornwall.' Corbett's own recipe for the best nutritional value advocated a mixture of rye grass, cocksfoot grass, rough-stalked meadow grass and red clover, but it did not suit every circumstance. The mixture was tried by several members of the Wadebridge Farmers' Club who found that it produced a heavier and coarser sward than was ideal for forage on their soil.

The second letter (transcribed and annotated in Appendix F) was written by Thomas to his son William in January 1844 and, for all that he is still the plantsman seeking ferns, mosses, shrubs and herbaceous plants for Pencarrow from New Zealand, and giving advice about how to get the best results from the clover and grass seeds that he had sent to Francis Molesworth in New Zealand the previous year, he shows himself to be an affectionate father and gives the impression that the family ties were close. William's sisters, Elizabeth and Mary, have clearly already written to William with the family news and told him that the hot-houses are 'complete in every particular', but Thomas breaks the news that his son now has a step-mother, telling William that his remarriage was 'absolutely necessary' for a man in his position and station, but it is not clear why William should be 'pleased and surprised' at his choice of wife. William's younger sister Mary is still at home and remains the 'Benjamin' of the family, but her elder sister has left home and, thanks to a family connection (and a payment of £30 from Thomas), Elizabeth (her temper much improved) is now apprenticed to a draper in London and can look forward to standing on her own feet, earning a respectable living (£20pa) at the end of her two years' apprenticeship. He encloses a paper (which has not survived) detailing the recent activities of the Wadebridge Farmers' Club (of which he was the founding secretary), and he rues the treatment that he has received with regard to his apparatus for heating hot-houses, principally at the hands of William Rendle, and regrets that he has not the funds to defend his rights and his patent in the courts; he informs William of the welcome arrival of a friendly young and like-minded 'scientific' farmer at Trescowe farm in place of the dreaded Tinney family with whom Thomas had obviously had a fearfully violent disagreement. Finally, he passes on good wishes from other employees at Pencarrow who had been friends with William and, in turn, asks to be remembered to two Pencarrow employees – James Bryant (who had served with him as a gardener) and John Tucker who had, like William, emigrated to New Zealand.

Thomas Corbett lived at a stimulating and exciting time for gardeners. It was an age in which there was a constant search for horticultural novelty and technical improvements in the science of cultivation. Head gardeners no longer worked in isolation; they were part of a network of gardeners anxious to promote horticulture as a 'scientific' discipline. In 1844, Corbett had paid his new neighbour at Trescowe the compliment of calling him a 'scientific' farmer, and nothing would have pleased him more than to be described as a 'scientific' gardener. There was ample opportunity for men such as Corbett to educate themselves and improve their knowledge and skills through the information, new ideas and experiences described in a plethora of gardening magazines which saw the light of day in the 1830s and 1840s.

Toby Musgrave in his *The Head Gardeners* (2007), quotes the following description in 1842 of two apprentice gardeners: the first 'was fond of mathematical studies, and liked well to talk about square roots, cube roots, equations, involutions of quantities, circles, angles, pyramids, cylinders, cones, polygons etc.' The second was 'in love with the study of natural history. He made himself pretty well acquainted with the botanical systems of Linnaeus and Jussieu: but he did not stop there, he acquired a knowledge of Cuvier's system of geology, Jameson's system of mineralogy, and an outline of geology.' Thomas Corbett could well have been an amalgam of both examples.

John Claudius Loudon was the first horticultural journalist, and he set the fashion when he published the first issue of The *Gardener's Magazine* in 1826, a monthly publication designed to 'disseminate new and important information on all topics connected with horticulture, and to raise the intellect and the character of those engaged in this art.' Loudon's periodical was followed by *The Gardener's Gazette*, *The Horticultural Magazine*, *The Horticultural Register*, *The Gardener*, *the Garden*, *Gardening Illustrated*, *Amateur Gardening*, *The Cottage Gardener* and *The Gardener's Chronicle* to name but a few. Of these the most influential, after *The Gardener's Magazine* ceased publication on Loudon's death in 1843, was *The Gardener's Chronicle* (later to be renamed *The Journal of Horticulture*), founded in 1841 by Joseph Paxton, the Duke of Devonshire's head gardener at Chatsworth. There can be little doubt that both periodicals, containing as they did, articles covering every conceivable aspect of gardening-information, comment, debate, latest plant introductions, new theories/developments and scientific reports were essential reading for Corbett, but he was not only interested in the esoteric and exotic aspects in gardening, the prosaic too was important, and we have a record of him purchasing a *Treatise on the Culture of Cucumbers, Melons, Sea-Kale & Asparagus*, published in 1840 by a Mr Smith.

As we have seen, Thomas Corbett's own contribution to some local and national horticultural debates was both sought and valued and, more-over, as a report in the West Briton in January 1841 attests, he was a 'talented lecturer.' At a meeting of the Farmers' Club of Probus, Cornwall, Corbett lectured, without notes, for two hours on 'The Physiology of Plants.' The lecture 'elicited the heartiest applause of a large and highly gratified audience who listened throughout with the greatest possible attention and interest.' Perhaps his interest and competence in the subject matter of his lecture can provide the clue to his sponsors' claim in 1829 that he was 'much attached to the study of Natural History,' particularly since in the course of the lecture Corbett described the system of classification of plants devised by Carl Linnaeus, the Swedish naturalist after whom the Linnean Society was named. It is worthy of note that part of the lecture was illustrated by 'some beautiful drawings, which were executed by the lecturer's two 'talented daughters.'

If the circumstances surrounding Thomas Corbett's election as an FLS are unclear, so too are the reasons behind the lapse of his Fellowship. The records of the Linnean Society merely record a 'withdrawal date' of 21 June 1842, but no reason is stated. He may have resigned because, living and working in Cornwall, he was unable to participate as much as he would have liked in the Society's affairs; it may have been that his subscription had become a luxury which he could not afford – we know from his letter to his son that he did not have money to spare, and records show that he had to ask his employer in July 1842 to pay 7 shillings for the repair of his 'mathematical instruments' – and yet, only a few months before his 'withdrawal', we find that he paid a subscription to the Benevolent Institute for the Relief of Aged & Indigent Gardeners & their Widows.

The debt that the gardens at Pencarrow owe to the inspiration, imagination and financial commitment of Sir William Molesworth has long been rightly acknowledged, but the contribution Thomas Corbett, the man who, as head gardener, plantsman and engineer, carried out his employer's designs has not been fully recognised. In 1848, Sir William visited Chatsworth, considered even then as the acme of country house gardens but, the grand conservatory apart, he was not impressed – 'the other hot-houses were not worth looking at' and he thought his own garden at Pencarrow was 'superior in beauty and form.' Sir William Molesworth had sought a 'really good gardener' to replace William Crawford. History shows that in Thomas Corbett he found the man he was looking for.

Notes & References

1   I am grateful to Mrs Susan Simmonds for providing this information.
2   The Grand Surrey Canal was opened in 1807 to link the Grand Surrey Docks, [a group of nine docks and six timber ponds on the south bank [the Surrey side] of the Thames created out of marshland on the Rotherhithe peninsula] to inland destinations. Designed to ship garden produce from Surrey to the London market, it proved a commercial failure, and no more than 3 ½ miles of canal were built.
3   Reproduced by kind permission of the Linnean Society.
4   William Edgcumbe Rendle (1820-81) originally a nurseryman from near Plymouth, he became a very successful entrepreneur who made a fortune by inventing form of glazing which was adopted by the government .
5   Excerpt from a speech by Sir William Molesworth advocating opportunities for all in the colonies.

Appendix A

Reproduced by kind permission from The Director's Correspondence, Royal Botanic Gardens, Kew, vol.16, f.90.

Appendix B

Pencarrow
11 Decbr 1841

Sir

I am directed by the members of the Wadebridge Farmers Club which is the largest and most influential society for the diffusion of Agricultural knowledge in Cornwall to apply to you for a collection of Grasses we have applied to several of the principal nurseries without success. The farmers in this county impressed with a conviction that the credits of the greater number of grasses are almost unknown are desirous of instituting a set of extensive and varied experements(*sic*) and I as their secretary am equally anxious to afford every assistance in my power to so laudable an undertaking I know of nothing of the kind that has been done since the experements(*sic*) of my late esteemed friend Mr Geo Sinclair at Woburn since his decease the subject has' almost ceased to call forth attention from any one and now as it is on the eve of being taken up in good earnest by farmers themselves I hope you will assist us in an undertaking so rational and so important to show you the ignorance (or worse) that prevail upon the subject I will only mention one circumstance viz I applied to three noted seedsmen in London who profess to have every good and almost every known sort for a small paper of Poa firtilis one of them replied there was no such thing the other that sent me a small paper each marked Poa firtilis one of which I believe to be some fusty old seed of Poa pratensis which never came up and the other proved to be Poa trivialis. Believing that you have an extensive and properly named collection at Kew and not being able to get them anywhere else I hope you will excuse the liberty we have taken in thus applying to you and should you be able to assist us in ever so small a degree you will confer a great honour on the members of this institution and probably a benefit on agriculture which will be highly valued I have the honour to be

Sir Wm

Your most Obt

& most humble Servt

Thos Corbett

Sir Wm Jackson Hooker Bart

Original letter is in the archive of the Royal Botanical Garden, Kew, Director's Correspondence vol.16, f.90.

Appendix C

SURNAME: CORBETT INITIALS: T TITLE: MR FORENAME: Thomas

ADDRESS1: Grand Surrey Docks OTHER NAME: SEX: Male

ADDRESS2: DEGREES:

ADDRESS3: HONOURS:

ADDRESS4: NATIONALITY: British

ADDRESS5: London

COUNTRY: England BIRTH DATE: DEATH DATE:

ELECT DATE: 2/2/1830 ADMIT DATE: REMOVAL DATE: WITHDRAWAL DATE: Omitted c.m 21/6/8-7

PORTRAIT: None MANUSCRIPT: None

LETTERS: None

MEMBER TYPE: FLS OTHER MEMBERSHIPS:

NOMINATED BY: G.Sinclair, G.Charlwood, T.Bell, J.C.Loudon G.T.Carey?

PLACE OF BURIAL: OBITUARY NOTICE:

PAST COMMITTEES:

MEDALS AND AWARDS:

PROFESSION: CAREER:

MAIN INTEREST:

The record of Thomas Corbett's service as a Fellow of the Linnean Society
(1830-1842)

Appendix D

Corbett's Advertisment Safeguarding his Patent System

Thomas Corbett begs leave to thank those Noblemen & Gentlemen & brother Gardeners who have so liberally patronised his system of Heating Horticultural Buildings of every description &, as it is rapidly becoming general, takes this method of apprising those who are not yet acquainted with his terms, that he requires $3 as a Patent Fee for every house so heated, on the receipt of which he will send a printed exposition of its entire principles, with any further instruction that may be wished, & a licence to have it erected by any tradesman his patron may think fit. It merits are considered to be efficiency, simplicity & cheapness. Thomas Corbett is also under the necessity of further stating that, as he is protected by His Majesty's Royal Letters Patent, he will rightly enforce the rights the Law allows him wherever these rights have been infringed.

Address – Thomas Corbett, Pencarrow, Bodmin, Cornwall

Published in *The Gardener's Chronicle* No.8, p.113, 20 February 1841.

Appendix E

Foliage above Ice-Houses

'As the earth is warmest in the Summer, being heated in great measure by radiant heat proceeding from the sun, it is at that period that the heat is transmitted from the surrounding earth to the ice-house with the greatest velocity; and the melting of the ice takes place in proportion to the difference in temperature between the stored ice and the surrounding medium. This difference is increased, either by the earth which surrounds the ice-house becoming heated by the rays of the sun, or by the freezing point of the ice becoming lowered by a mixture of salt. It is, therefore, a desirable object to keep the surrounding earth as cool as possible. If the ice-house is surrounded and overtopped with large trees, their effects will be – first, To shield off the rays of the sun from the earth below; and secondly, The great surface of foliage exposed to the light and air, will be continually giving off water in the form of vapour, which, in the transformation of water into vapour, will have taken up 950deg.(F) of heat in a latent state, more than the water contained, and expanded into about 1,600 times its former volume, having in effect destroyed about 950deg. of sensible heat for all the water given off, (the quantity of which is known to be very great in hot and very dry weather). A coolness is therefore produced under the shade of the large trees which is not to be found in exposed situations, produced, it may be presumed, not only from the shade of their foliage, but from the evaporation of water from their surfaces; but the still air beneath being an excellent non-conductor, the earth below will be found to be several degrees colder than that which is exposed. Again, the drip of the trees from accumulated dew etc., instead of being injurious, must be beneficial, because the surface of the soil will be partially wet when that of exposed ground will be quite dry. The evaporation from the surface will produce a coldness below. But it may be said, that though the mere surface of the earth under large trees is often damp when exposed surfaces are dry, yet the earth below is much dryer under and about the roots of large trees than anywhere else. This I consider a great advantage: dry earth is a much better non-conductor of heat than wet; and I contend that the rain that falls where large trees are is evaporated in a larger proportion from the surface than if it fell in an exposed situation. It appears to me that the best of all places for an ice-house is the side of a hill covered with large trees, three-fourths of the house being sunk beneath the surface of the ground, and the top being covered with earth and planted with ivy.'

Corbett's opinion cited by Charles MacIntosh in *The Garden* (1853), pp. 503-4.

Pencarrow
22d Jany 1844

My Dear William

     I gladly received your letter written three days after you arrived in New Zealand but months have now passed away and no other has yet come to hand which makes us feel very anxious to hear from you and particularly after the deplorable news from Nelson[i] and other indications of insubordination among the natives I hope however by the time you receive this that things will be more settled and increased prosperity attend all the colonies of NZ. I hope you are still serving Mr Francis[ii] faithfully and energetically and don't join with the grumblers we are anxiously looking for specimens of plants mosses Ferns. Ferns if possible with fructification three parts ripe and specimens of any handsome shrub or herbasious(*sic*) plant that you may get seeds of have you any handsome insects to send us or the skins of birds cured with pepper and arsenic. I hope you have written full accts of all your proceedings which I may shortly receive. Elizabeth and Mary[iii] have I believe told you all the news with us which will save me the trouble I send you a paper with an acct of our Club[iv]. I daresay you will be rather pleased as well as surprised at the choice I have made of a Wife[v] which was an absolutely necessary part of my establishment she desires her kindest love to you and is extremely anxious to hear from you I have got Eliza[be]th I hope into a line of doing well she had a great desire to be a draper and I got her into an excellent shop in London where I paid 30£ with her for two years after which I have no doubt she will be able to earn her 20£ a year and board in a respectable way she is exceedingly clever she has completely conquered her original bad temper and they are very fond of her. Her master is Mr Constable who married Miss Jane Greenwood of Devonport cousin to our Jane[vi] her address is Miss Corbett Mr Constable 202 Tottenham Court Road London she wrote you some time ago but you may not have received her letter Mary is still the pet bird at home and we are all extremely comfortable we have got a very nice neighbour at Trescowe Mr Olver[vii] a young scientific farmer with whom you may suppose I am very intimate my life was threatened by the Tinny's[viii] (*sic*) but I believe they were too much afraid of their own precious necks to carry their threats into expectation. My hotwater licences[ix] are quite stopped Rendle[x] has advertised everywhere that it is his invention and no one has a right to pay me and as he is a constant advertiser in the Gardeners Chronical(*sic*) to the tune of about 100£ a year with his puffery it is all now called Rendles tank system and I have never moved to contradict it as I have no money to go to law and the time-serving Dr Lindley[xi] holds now all the Gardening news in his own hand poor Loudon[xii] is dead please remember me to Mr Molesworth and also to Bryant & Tucker.[xiii] Mr Mclean[xiv] desires his very kind regards to(*sic*) he is extremely kind and always enquires after you - as also Mr Lakeman[xx]. Mr Mitchinson[xvi] also desired me to remember him in the kindest way to you and also to Bryant you do not say how many children they have is he steady is he still a Tea-totler(*sic*) or has he taken to drinking John Cleave[xvii] and Charles the groom[xviii] are both Tea-totlers(*sic*) by Sir Wms Orders I think Mary has explained to you about the Hothouses. They are very complete in every particular I think you should mention in your letters if there is anything we could send in a small way that would be of use what seeds. I sent some Clover and Grass seeds in the last ship for Mr Molesworth they should be sown separately on very clean ground to get the seeds from each pure they would supply the other land with seed but it should be kept particularly clean I should like to know how the different clovers and grasses do with you and I will send more seeds of any that does well if there is any room in the Box in which this is going I will send a little garden seed of some plants for Mr M

I am

My Dearest Boy

Your Affectionate Father

Thos Corbett

Are there any shells?

The original letter is in the Turnbull Library, Wellington, New Zealand

i   In June 1843, there was a serious clash of arms at Wairau, near Nelson, in the north of South Island between Maori natives and British settlers from the New Zealand Company. Several people on both sides were killed in the incident which became known as the Wairau Affray/Massacre.

ii   Francis Molesworth, the younger brother of Sir William Molesworth 8th Bt., who emigrated to New Zealand in 1839, but returned to England in 1844 for medical reasons and died, unmarried, aged twenty-eight in 1846.

iii   Elizabeth and Mary, Corbett's daughters from his marriage to Elizabeth Maughan. At the time of writing, they were aged nineteen and sixteen respectively.

iv   Almost certainly a reference to the Wadebridge Farmers' Club.

v   Elizabeth Jane Greenwood, the daughter of the local inn-keeper at Washaway, whom he married 30 May 1843, six months after the death of his first wife.

vi   Unidentifiable.

vii   Thomas Olver, the aged thirty. By 1861, he was farming 500 acres and employing 10 men, 5 boys and 4 women.

viii   Ralph Tinney, his wife Elizabeth and their nine children. The threats and their origin are a mystery.

ix   A reference to Corbett's 'hygrothermatic' system for heating hot-houses.

x   William Edgecumbe Rendle (1820-81). Started life as a nurseryman in his father's business in Plymouth and invented a 'tank system for heating horticultural buildings' very similar to Corbett's invention but which, because of his greater financial standing, he was able to market aggressively to the detriment of Corbett's system.

xi   John Lindley (1799-1865), Botanist and horticulturalist. Professor of botany in the University of London and a founder of the Gardeners' Chronicle in 1841 – a journal which Corbett considered discriminated unfairly against him and his invention.

xii   John Claudius Loudon (1783-1843), The leading horticultural writer of his day with whose writings Corbett was familiar.

xiii   James Bryant (1812-1902) a gardener at Pencarrow 1833-1839 when, after marrying his wife Mary Anne, a domestic servant at Pencarrow, he emigrated to New Zealand with Francis Molesworth.
        Tucker - .members of the Tucker family were employed at Pencarrow and were, at the time of writing, living in one of the Pencarrow cottages, but the emigrant cannot be identified for certain.

xiv   Duncan McLean (1801-74), Sir William Molesworth's manservant and later butler.

xv   John Lakeman (*c.*1801-80). Steward and land agent for the Pencarrow estate. Lived with his family at Costislost.

xvi   Unidentifiable.

xvii   John Cleave, manservant to the young Sir William in 1824; at the time of writing was the coachman at Pencarrow.

xviii   Unidentifiable.

Aubrey Bartlett, Head gardener (1898-1910)

Aubrey Bartlett was the Head Gardener at Pencarrow from 1898 until shortly after the death in 1910 of his employer, Mrs Mary Ford. She was the sister of Sir William Molesworth Bart. (1810-55), who designed and laid out the gardens, made the rockery and planted a great number and variety of the trees in the 1830s and 1840s. But, for all Sir William's innovative planting and creative horticultural genius which was much admired in his lifetime, it was Bartlett, sixty years later, who was in charge of the heyday of the gardens, and his reputation as a gardener was well-established by the time he was featured in October 1903 at the age of thirty-one as no.105 in *The Garden Life's* series of famous gardeners.

Aubrey Bartlett was born in 1872. His father was the bailiff and gardener of the Knightleys estate on St. David's Hill, Exeter, and Bartlett

Knightleys estate, Exeter. (demolished 1902)

started his apprenticeship here under his father at about the age of twelve. He moved to another estate in Exeter, Parker's Well, at Heavitree in 1885 to further his training, before moving to Dropmore Park in Buckinghamshire in 1888. He spent seven years here, latterly as foreman under the head gardener Mr Herrin, to whom Bartlett readily admitted he was greatly indebted. In 1895, he then went to gain further experience for two years as a student gardener at Kew Gardens, where he attracted the attention of William Watson, the Assistant Curator, who recommended him in 1898 as well-suited for the post of head gardener at Pencarrow. Between Kew and his arrival at Pencarrow, Bartlett spent a season at Finsbury Park, Haringey, one of the first great London parks laid out in the Victorian era, to gain, as he put it, 'an insight into that branch of gardening.'

Finsbury Park, where Bartlett "gained insight" into large-scale gardening

His experience at Dropmore, where there was a fine *pinetum*, and at Kew where William Watson, a renowned expert in the cultivation of orchids, had shared his expertise with him, made Bartlett's move to Pencarrow a very logical appointment, since trees, pines in particular, and orchids had been the overriding passions of Sir William Molesworth. Bartlett was also a frequent contributor to horticultural journals, principally *The Gardener's Chronicle*, and he greatly assisted Henry J. Elwes in providing material for his *Trees of Great Britain* (1905). Elwes showed his gratitude by giving conifer seedlings from his own estate (Colesborne Park in Gloucestershire) for planting at Pencarrow. Although most of Bartlett's contributions to the horticultural journals were on the subject of trees - of the instances which I have come across he wrote about the *picea morinda, the taxodium distichum*, the *fagus betuloides*, the *ulnus campestris* and, predictably, the *araucaria imbricata* a tree closely associated with Pencarrow, and first named the 'monkey puzzle tree' there when it was planted at the foot of the rockery by Sir William in 1834. In 1899 he wrote that this specimen had grown to a height of 20m, and had become something of a phenomenon in as much as it was monoecious, bearing both female 'cones' and male 'catkins.' Other aspects of nature prompted Bartlett's to write to the press: in 1906, for example, he wrote to *The Gardeners' Chronicle* about a passion for eating tomatoes which he had observed in male, but never in hen, blackbirds, and he had also noticed a craving the pheasants at Pencarrow had acquired for eating gunnera leaves - but he noted that the pheasants were pernickety, clearly preferring the flavour of the leaves of *gunnera scabra* to the taste of *gunnera manicata*!

Mrs Ford was determined to follow her brother's initiatives by maintaining the estate and replacing dead and damaged trees, and there is an impressive list of the plantings Bartlett carried out for her in the last decade of her life.

Most of the planting involved trees, but shrubs, especially rhododendrons, also featured. Bartlett took pride in the azaleas, rhododendrons, camellias which flourished in the American garden beyond the lake, and he was also responsible for the four acres of the kitchen garden, the hot houses and the Italian garden, the two acres of flower garden to the south of the house, into which he introduced annually some twelve thousand bedding plants selected to flower from July onwards to coincide with his employers annual summer visit to Pencarrow

With the death of Mary Ford in 1910, the house and garden passed to Sir Lewis Molesworth, the 11th baronet, who not only did not want to live at Pencarrow, but made it known that he intended to abandon the outer kitchen garden, do away with the beds and bedding plants in the Italian garden and, as he wrote to the family solicitor, 'spend as little as possible on the house and garden.'

There was even a possibility of 'letting the gardener's house, part of the garden and the cow fields' to a tenant, but nothing came of it. Nevertheless, the writing was on the wall for Bartlett since the economies and limitations envisaged by Sir Lewis would greatly diminish the importance and influence of the head gardener. As soon as he learned of Sir Lewis's intentions, Bartlett requested a testimonial to allow him to be free to seek a new horticultural challenge. He left Pencarrow shortly afterwards, and there is no record of the appointment of a replacement head gardener in the years before Sir Hugh Molesworth-St. Aubyn and his family came to live at Pencarrow after WWI.

After leaving Pencarrow, Bartlett took up a position in Surrey before taking over a market garden in Hampton, Middlesex, but illness compelled him to give up commercial gardening. He maintained his gardening interests, however, by acting in an advisory capacity (especially in connection with trees) and by contributing articles to gardening journals. He was employed by *The Gardeners' Chronicle* to report on the shows staged by Royal Horticultural Society for nearly forty years until his death in 1950 and for some years, he acted as Secretary to the National Dahlia Society and the National Sweet Pea Society. He was affectionately known as 'Uncle Bartlett' by the children in the care of the Royal Gardeners' Orphan Fund of which he became Secretary in 1925. During WW2 he acted as horticultural advisor to the London Command and, according to his obituary published in *The Gardeners' Chronicle*, he could have held military rank if he had so wished. His obituary describes Aubrey Bartlett as "very likeable, quaintly humorous, knowledgeable, even-tempered and a lover of poetry." I like to think that he will have valued and enjoyed his years at Pencarrow. I know he will have been proud of his contribution to British horticulture which was recognized in 1947 when the Council of the Royal Horticultural Society made him an Associate of Honour.

Araucaria araucana, **the monkey puzzle tree.**
A conifer once much in evidence at Pencarrow. The seeds were first introduced to this country by William Lobb, the plant hunter, in 1844.

Pencarrow Lake

A spring-fed stream naturally winds its way through the American gardens down the valley from the south towards the mansion of Pencarrow. Its flow is interrupted and regulated by a man-made dam creating an upper lake which, together with another spring, feeds a lower basin. The earliest pictorial record of Pencarrow, a painting by an unknown artist c.1770, suggests that the stream then flowed naturally into a pond, in a hollow, just beyond the southern end of what is now known as the Italian garden, before disappearing underground on its way to run into the river Camel. No such stretch of water is marked near the mansion on the first Ordnance Survey map of 1813, although the lake and the basin are shown (Figure 1), and both water features are clearly marked in the 1840 tithe map of the parish of Egloshayle (Figure 2), in which it also appears that there may have been two further ponds at the northern limit of what was to become the American gardens later in the nineteenth century.

The mansion at Pencarrow was extensively renovated/restored/rebuilt by the 4th and 5th Molesworth baronets c.1765-1775, and it has long been thought that the work which was undertaken at that time - the height of the popularity of designed landscapes in the country estates of the aristocracy and landed gentry - was limited to the house, and that the improvements were not extended to the park and gardens since, if the gardens had been landscaped at this time, they would almost certainly have included an ornamental water feature readily accessible and visible from the house to enliven the scenery and act as a source of entertainment. The lake and the basin, man-made as they are, may well have been visible from the house when they were constructed, but neither map shows that they were easily accessible, and neither was sufficiently extensive to support the sort of fashionable water-based entertainment of that period.

As it is, we know of no work being undertaken in the area of the lake until 1843, when Sir William Molesworth, the 8th baronet, in 1843, began to reshape the valley beyond the Italian garden and rockery which he had created in the 1830s. Although there are some records of the planting in and around the lake (often referred to less impressively by Sir William and others as a pond), the lake itself was not a feature worthy of mention in the accounts of Pencarrow by Twycross (1846), Burke (1853) or Lake (1867), nor was it recorded in the first detailed account of Sir William's innovations and future landscape plans at Pencarrow which appeared in an article above the initials WFR in the *Gardeners' Chronicle* in August 1842. It is not until January 1878 that a reference to the lake is recorded in an article by Edward Luckhurst published in the *Journal of Horticulture and Cottage Gardener*, one in a series of *Notes from Cornish Gardens*. Luckhurst was greatly impressed by what he saw at Pencarrow, describing the developments as 'one of the finest examples of landscape gardening in the country', and he was particularly taken with his walk up the valley from the rockery past a 'fine piece of water where the banks are very high and steep,' and where the paths 'wind picturesquely around the water to the crowning glory of the valley, a rhododendron garden some two acres in extent.' Puzzlingly, Luckhurst made no mention of the lower lake/basin, nor does he mention the two ponds at the southern head of the American gardens. The former was certainly still in existence, but perhaps the ponds had already been filled in, either to improve the flow of water to the lake or, possibly, to make the most of the rhododendron garden

Sir William Molesworth intended the lake to be a focal point separating the two halves of the American garden he created. There are indications that he stocked the lake with ducks (he refers to the lake as a duck pond in a letter to his sister, Mary, in July 1844) or, as an article in *The Gardeners' Magazine* in February 1909 suggests 'rare aquatic birds' which were acclimatised in the fowl-house below the lake. It is also likely that Sir William stocked the lake with fish since there is in the Pencarrow archive a photograph of 1868 capturing a Miss Lister, Lady Diana Beauclerk, and Mr Borthwick, house guests of Sir William's widow, Lady Andalusia Molesworth, sitting holding fishing-rods on the south-west bank of the lake (Figure 3). Sir William's planting book reveals that the lake itself was planted in 1843 with the following aquatic plants: *Aponogeton distachyos* (Cape pondweed from South Africa); *Acorus calamus* (sweet flags from America); *Butomus umbellatus* (flowering rush from the UK); *Menyanthus trifoliate* (buck bean from the UK); *Spergula nodosa* (pearlwort spurrey from the UK); *Amaryllis longifolia* (water lily from South Africa) and, later on (1909) large groups of arum lilies were a feature. In the early 1840s the lower half of the American garden was planted with various species of gunnera, irises, pampas grass, sedges, bullrushes, bamboo and New Zealand flax, together with choice conifers, eucalyptus, elm and holm oak trees. Early in 1848, the Sir William records planting the head of the 'pond' with rhododendrons and a granite seat was made there. In the autumn, the walk to the second half of the American garden was improved and planted with laurels and a hedge of sweet briar. Also a number of magnolias were planted – *grandiflora, Soulangeana, conspicua, tripetala, acuminata, glauca, purpurea, Hammondii* – and among the many pine varieties planted were: *insignis, patula, Hartwegi, Gerardiana, Lambertiana, Laricio, serolina, inops virginiana, ponderosa and mitis echinata.*

Further significant planting was undertaken in the area of the lake by Aubrey Bartlett, the head gardener (1899-1912) during the years when Mrs Mary Ford, the sister of the 8th baronet, was the chatelaine of Pencarrow. Particularly important and relevant was the planting of the two wing-nut trees (*pterocarya fraxinifolia* from Caucasia and *pterocarya stenoptera* from China) on the top of the dam itself. They are very handsome, ornamental deciduous trees with long dangling racemes of thick green flowers. However, although these trees have proved a very attractive feature above ground for the past hundred years, their roots were the cause of the leak in the south-west corner of the dam and they had to be felled and the roots ground out in the autumn of 2006. The dam has now been repaired and access to the lake has been greatly improved thanks to the funding by the Friends of Pencarrow. The wing-nuts were planted in 1907, and so just failed to reach their centenary, but their disappearance has not only helped to secure the wall of the dam, it has also opened up a vista in the grounds which has not been seen since early in the last century.

Fishing Party at Pencarrow Lake, 1868

173

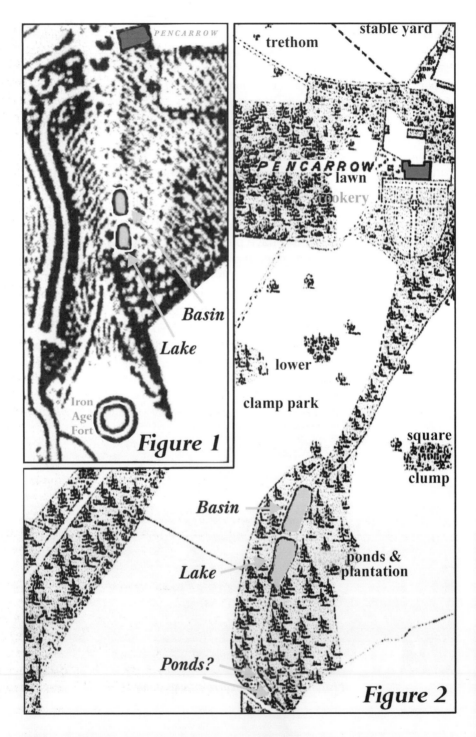

PENCARROW

Basin

Lake

Iron Age Fort

Figure 1

stable yard

trethom

P E N C A R R O W
lawn
rookery

lower

clamp park

square
clump

Basin

Lake

ponds &
plantation

Ponds?

Figure 2